BOOK 2

Topics FROM A TO Z

Steps to Success in Listening and Speaking

Irene E. Schoenberg

Longman

Topics from A to Z, Book 2:
Steps to Success in Listening and Speaking

Pearson Education, 10 Bank Street,
White Plains, NY 10606

Vice president of multimedia and skills: Sherry Preiss
Executive editor: Laura Le Drean
Development manager: Paula Van Ells
Development editors: John Barnes / Debbie Sistino
Senior production editor: Robert Ruvo
Director of manufacturing: Patrice Fraccio
Senior manufacturing buyer: Nancy Flaggman
Photo research: Tara Maldonado
Cover design: Stuart Goldstein
Text design: 2AM Diseño
Text composition: 2AM Diseño
Text font: 11/14 Times Roman
Illustrations: Luis Briseño / 2AM Diseño

Text Credits: **page 73** *OVER THE RAINBOW*, By: Harold Arlen and E.Y.
Harburg © 1938 (Renewed 1966) Metro-Goldwyn-Mayer Inc. © 1939
(Renewed 1967) EMI Feist Catalog Inc., Rights Throughout the World
Controlled by EMI Feist Catalog Inc. (Publishing) And Warner Bros.
Publications U.S. Inc. (Print), All Rights Reserved. Used by Permission.
WARNER BROS. PUBLICATIONS U.S. INC., Miami, FL 33014; **page 93**
From *Phenomenal Woman* © 1978 by Maya Angelou from *AND STILL
I RISE* by Maya Angelou. Used by permission from Random House Inc.
Reproduced from *AND STILL I RISE* by Maya Angelou, by permission of
Virago Press, a division of Time Warner Book Group UK.

Photo Credits: **page 6** (left) © Jonelle Weaver/GettyImages; (center) ©
David Kelly Crow/Photo Edit; (right) © SuperStock, Inc.; **page 13** (left)
© Peter Turnley/CORBIS; (right) © Jacqui Hurst/CORBIS; **page 17**
(left) © Bettmann/CORBIS; (right) © Bettmann/CORBIS; **page 25** (left)
© Duomo/CORBIS; (right) © Rufus F. Folkks/CORBIS; **page 26** (left)
© Duomo/CORBIS; (center) © David Stoecklein/CORBIS; (right) ©
Bettmann/CORBIS; **page 29** (top) © Duomo/CORBIS; (left) © Duomo/
CORBIS; (center) © Duomo/CORBIS; (right) © Kim Kyung-Hoon/

Reuters/Corbis; **page 30** (top) © Chel Beeson/Index Stock Imagery; (left)
© Aldo Torelli/GettyImages; (center left) © Keren Su/CORBIS; (center
right) © Scott T. Baxter/GettyImages; (right) © Royalty-Free/CORBIS;
page 33 © Eric Meola/GettyImages; **page 34** (left) © Rita Maas/
GettyImages; (center) © Brian Hagiwara/GettyImages; (right) © Jonelle
Weaver/GettyImages; **page 38** (top) © AP/Wide World Photos; (left) ©
Reuters/CORBIS; (center left) © Steve Vidler/eStockPhoto/PictureQuest;
(center right) © Images.com/CORBIS; (right) © Christine Osbourne/
CORBIS; **page 41** © John Van Hasselt/CORBIS SYGMA; **page 42** (top)
© Glen Davison / Index Stock Imagery; (left) © Photo Index / Image Stock
Imagery; (center left) © Charles Philip/CORBIS; (center right) © Paul
A. Sauders/CORBIS; (right) © SLOCOMB JEFF/CORBIS SYGMA;
page 45 (top) © Mark Segal / Index Stock Imagery; (bottom) © Sam
Wilkinson/GettyImages; **page 50** (left) 20th Century Fox/Paramount/The
Kobal Connection; (center) © Jim Lake/CORBIS; (right) © Royalty-Free/
CORBIS; **page 58** (top) © Royalty-Free/CORBIS; (left) © Yann Arthus-
Bertrand/CORBIS; (center) © Royalty-Free/CORBIS; (right) © Reuters/
CORBIS; **page 61** © Smithsonian American Art Museum, Washington,
DC / Art Resource, NY; **page 77** (top left) (top center) (top right); (bottom
left) © Bettmann/CORBIS; (bottom center) © Christie's Images/CORBIS;
(bottom right) © Museum of Flight/CORBIS; **page 78** (left) © Royalty-
Free/CORBIS; (center) © Edward Bock/CORBIS; (right) © Bettmann/
CORBIS; **page 81** (top) © Edward Bock/CORBIS; **page 82** (left) Royalty-
Free/CORBIS; (center) © Gavriel Jecan/CORBIS; (right) © Reuters/
CORBIS; **page 85** © 2004 Artists Rights Society (ARS) New York/
ADAGP, Paris; digital image © The Museum of Modern Art/Licensed by
SCALA / Art; **page 86** (left) © Jonathan Blair/CORBIS; (center) © Tom
Stewart/CORBIS; (right) © Grayce Roessler/ Index Stock Imagery;
page 88 © Amy and Chuck Wiley/Wales/ Index Stock Imagery; **page 89**
(left) © Royalty-Free/CORBIS; (right) © Royalty-Free/CORBIS; **page 90**
© (left) Bettmann/CORBIS; (center left) © AP/Wide World Photos; (center
right); **page 93** (top) © Christopher Felver/CORBIS; (bottom) © Francis
G. Mayer/CORBIS; **page 94** (top) © Fotomorgana/CORBIS; (center left)
© Banana Stock Royalty Free/Fotosearch; (center right) © Royalty-Free/
CORBIS; (right) © Royalty-Free/CORBIS; **page 98** (top left) © Royalty-
Free/CORBIS; (top right) © Digital Vision/Getty Images; (bottom left)
© Royalty Free/Comstock; (center) © Philip Habib/Image Bank/ Getty
Images; (bottom right) © Fabrizio Cacciatore/ Index Stock Imagery;
page 105 (top) © Source: Totes-Isotoner Corp.

Library of Congress Cataloging-in-Publication Data

Schoenberg, Irene
 Topics from A to Z. Book 2 / Irene Schoenberg.
   p. cm.
 ISBN 0-13-185076-8
 1. English language--Textbooks for foreign speakers. 2. English language--Spoken English--Problems,
exercises, etc. 3. Conversation--Problems, exercises, etc. 4. Listening--Problems, exercises, etc. I. Title.
PE1128.S346 2005
428.3'4--dc22

2004016514

ISBN: 0-13-185076-8

Printed in the United States of America
1 2 3 4 5 6 7 8 9 10 VHJ 09 08 07 06 05 04

Contents

Unit 1	Air Travel	2
Unit 2	Breakfast	6
Unit 3	Colors	10
Unit 4	Days, Months, and Numbers	14
Unit 5	E-mail and the Internet	18
Unit 6	Fears and Phobias	22
Unit 7	Games and Sports	26
Unit 8	Holidays and Special Occasions	30
Unit 9	Ice Cream and Other Desserts	34
Unit 10	Jazz and Other Types of Music	38
Unit 11	Kangaroos, Koalas, and Australia	42
Unit 12	Love	46
Unit 13	Movies	50
Unit 14	Newspapers	54
Unit 15	Oceans and Beaches	58
Unit 16	Parties	62
Unit 17	Quizzes, Tests, and Intelligence	66
Unit 18	Rain	70
Unit 19	Sisters and Brothers	74
Unit 20	Telephones	78
Unit 21	Urban and Rural Areas	82
Unit 22	Vacations	86
Unit 23	Women	90
Unit 24	X-rays and Bones	94
Unit 25	Years Ago: Childhood Memories	98
Unit 26	Zippers, Buttons, and Velcro: Clothes and Fashion	102
Tapescript		109

Scope and Sequence

Unit	Title	Functions	Listening
1 Page 2	*Air Travel*	Exchanging information and expressing preferences about air travel	1. Flight Delays and Cancellations 2. A Bargain Flight to Miami
2 Page 6	*Breakfast*	Discussing breakfast habits; Expressing opinions about breakfast	1. Ordering Breakfast in a Restaurant 2. Breakfast Habits in Japan
3 Page 10	*Colors*	Exchanging information about color preferences; Sharing opinions about colors	1. Describing One's Appearance 2. Color and Food
4 Page 14	*Days, Months, and Numbers*	Talking about lucky numbers, favorite days and seasons; Exchanging opinions about days, months, and seasons	1. Listening for a Phone Number and Address 2. Coincidences: Two Presidents
5 Page 18	*E-mail and the Internet*	Exchanging information about computer use; Sharing opinions about computers, the Internet, and e-mail	1. Origin of "Computer Bug" 2. Checking Medical Problems on the Internet
6 Page 22	*Fears and Phobias*	Discussing fears and phobias; Exchanging opinions about fear	1. Trying to Learn a Sport 2. Advice About Shyness
7 Page 26	*Games and Sports*	Exchanging information about favorite sports and games; Sharing opinions about sports and games	1. Facts About the Olympics 2. Tiger Woods
8 Page 30	*Holidays and Special Occasions*	Discussing likes and dislikes about holidays; sharing opinions about holidays	1. Choosing a Birthday Gift 2. Holiday Stress
9 Page 34	*Ice Cream and Other Desserts*	Exchanging information about sweets and desserts; Sharing opinions about desserts	1. Ingredients for a Cake 2. Facts About Ice Cream
10 Page 38	*Jazz and Other Types of Music*	Discussing musical preferences; Expressing opinions about music	1. Five Famous Pieces of Music 2. Brazilian Music
11 Page 42	*Kangaroos, Koalas, and Australia*	Exchanging information and opinions about Australia	1. The Sydney Opera House 2. Facts About Uluru
12 Page 46	*Love*	Discussing Romance; Expressing opinions about love and marriage	1. Describing A Potential Boyfriend 2. A Romantic Problem
13 Page 50	*Movies*	Exchanging information and sharing opinions about movies	1. Different Kinds of Movies 2. Two Successful Films

Pronunciation Pointer	Conversation Practice	Check This Out
Content Words and Function Words	Information Gap: Choosing a Flight	Cartoon: Time Travel
Rising Intonation for *Yes/No* Questions	Role Play: Ordering from a Menu	Breakfast of the Future
Stress to Show Meaning	Correcting Wrong Information	Color Preferences and Personality
Syllables	Getting Information about Important Phone Numbers and addresses	Math puzzles
/i/ and /ɪ/	Words with Two Meanings	Cartoon: "You've Got Mail!"
Stress on *too* and *either*	Describing Experiences about Overcoming Fears	Phobias of Famous People
Thirteen or thirty?	Information Gap: The Olympics	Earnings of Athletes
Rising and Falling Intonation for Choice Questions	Asking and Answering Choice Questions	Holiday Dress of Dogon in West Africa
Stress in Compound Nouns	Vocabulary Practice: Types of Food	Comparing Dessert Presentation
Rhythm	Talking about "Background Music"	Astrud Gilberto: Brazilian singer
Can and Can't	Facts about kangaroos and other animals	Rock Art
/l/ and /r/	Describing Good Friends	Symbols of love
Sounds that Have Meaning	Using Sounds to Express Opinions	Chart: Attitudes about Movies

Scope and Sequence

Unit	Title	Functions	Listening
14 Page 54	*Newspapers*	Sharing information and opinions about newspapers and other news sources	1. Origin of the word *News* 2. Radio News Broadcast
15 Page 58	*Oceans and Beaches*	Discussing favorite activities at the beach; Sharing opinions about beaches	1. A Trip to the Beach 2. How to Relax
16 Page 62	*Parties*	Sharing information and opinions about parties	1. Phone Messages 2. Party "Ice Breakers"
17 Page 66	*Quizzes, Tests, and Intelligence*	Discussing test preferences; Exchanging opinions about tests	1. Quiz Show 2. Different Kinds of Intelligence
18 Page 70	*Rain*	Talking about weather-related experiences; Sharing opinions about the rain	1. A Weather Report 2. Forecasting the Weather
19 Page 74	*Sisters and Brothers*	Discussing families and sibling relationships; Expressing opinions about children	1. Only Children 2. The Brontë Sisters
20 Page 78	*Telephones*	Sharing information, preferences, and opinions about phones	1. Choosing a Message for an Answering Machine 2. Ad for a Picture Phone
21 Page 82	*Urban and Rural Areas*	Talking about experiences in urban and rural areas; Exchanging opinions about living in a city or the country	1. Describing an Apartment 2. City Life vs. Country Life
22 Page 86	*Vacations*	Discussing vacation preferences; Sharing opinions about vacations	1. Going Camping 2. Tours to Bryce Canyon and Machu Picchu
23 Page 90	*Women*	Talking about gender roles; Sharing opinions about men and women	1. Advice to Women about Salaries 2. Poem by Maya Angelou
24 Page 94	*X-rays and Bones*	Finding out classmates' experiences with broken bones; Exchanging opinions about bones	1. Pirate Flags 2. X-Rays
25 Page 98	*Years Ago: Childhood Memories*	Sharing information about childhood memories; Giving opinions about childhood	1. What Game are the Children Playing? 2. Museum of Childhood Memories
26 Page 102	*Zippers, Buttons, and Velcro: Clothes and Fashion*	Talking about shopping and clothes; Exchanging opinions about the importance of clothes	1. Complimenting People on Their Clothes 2. The Story of the Zipper

Pronunciation Pointer	Conversation Practice	Check This Out
/dʒ/ and /tʃ/	Talking about Current Events	Famous Headlines from the Past
/ou/ and /ɔ/	Beach Vocabulary: Word Games and Storytelling	Comparing a Winslow Homer painting and a John Masefield poem
Linking Words	Talking about Party Invitations	Dressing Up for Parties
Plural endings /s/, /z/, and /ɪz/	Vocabulary Game: /ɪz/ endings	Brain Teaser: How many triangles?
Sentence Stress in Limericks	Information Gap: Weather in Different Cities	Somewhere Over the Rainbow
Reduction of *and*	Talking about Relatives	Famous Siblings
/t/(*ten*), /θ/ (*three*), and /ð/ (*the*)	Completing Telephone Conversations	Cartoon: Cell Phones
Statements as Questions	Talking about Ideal Homes	Marc Chagall Painting: *I and the Village*
/p/, /b/, /v/, and /f/	Packing for a camping trip	Shopping While on Vacation
Irregular Plural Nouns	Talking about men's and women's earnings	Comparing a Georges Seurat Painting and a Maya Angelou Poem
Stress in Abbreviations	Idioms with the word "bone"	Medical symbols
The /w/ sound	Talking about Childhood Games	Cartoon: Childhood Memories
Stress on the Final Word in a Sentence	Talking about Fasteners: Zippers and Velcro	Cartoon: Hairstyles

Preface

Topics from A to Z, Book 2 is the second of a conversation/listening series written for beginning to low-intermediate level adult and young adult students. Each text contains 26 four-page units, one for each letter of the alphabet. Each unit consists of Facts, Talk about Your Experience, Give Your Opinion, Pronunciation Pointer, Listening Comprehension 1 and 2, Conversation Practice, and Check It Out. Authentic art, poetry, music, and photographs help to maintain student interest throughout the text.

Opening Art

Each unit starts with an engaging piece of art and an accompanying question that get students involved in the unit's content. For example, in Unit 1, "Air Travel," students look at four illustrations of people waiting at an airport and consider what they would do in that situation. In Unit 6, "Fears and Phobias," students see illustrations of people's greatest fears and consider their own.

Facts

In this section, groups of students work together trying to answer 5 or 6 multiple choice or true/false questions. Illustrations with labels help students understand new words. Some questions are language-based, aiming to increase students' knowledge of words and phrases. Others are fun facts about the context. For example, Unit 1, "Air Travel," includes these questions:

Were you right?

1. After traveling a long distance in a plane, many people have jet _____.   _____

   a. lag   b. set   c. dreams

2. The first flight attendants were single, female _____.   _____

   a. cooks   b. teachers   c. nurses

3. In 1987 American Airlines saved $40,000. The airline stopped putting _____   _____
   in each salad in first class.

   a. an olive   b. a tomato   c. a carrot

Next, students listen to the facts and compare them to their guesses. Finally, students read the facts aloud and try to remember them. Some will remember all the facts; others will remember only one or two. In time students discover their own learning style. Some write the sentences or take notes. Others read them several times. Some work alone. Others prefer to work with a partner.

Language experts generally agree that students learn best when they focus on, repeat, and try to remember an item. Memory is thus a key to language improvement. In this section students develop their skills at memorizing interesting and helpful content.

Talk about Your Experience

In this part, students work with a partner to give personal answers to a set of guided questions. Even the most reticent student can participate in this activity. For example, in Unit 6 students ask each other the following:

	YOU	YOUR PARTNER

• As a child, did you have any special fears (for example, a fear of the dark)?
• When did you stop being afraid?
• When you are afraid, what happens to your body?
  • Does your heart beat fast?
  • Do you sweat?
  • Do you scream?		

After students have spoken with a partner, a class discussion or a survey gets students to talk to a larger group. The language is controlled, the topics are non-threatening, and the result is that the whole class becomes involved. For example, in the unit on Fears and Phobias, students ask five classmates these questions:

Is it easy for you to:	Yes	No	Sometimes
a. start a conversation with someone you've just met?	☐	☐	☐
b. enter a room when most people are seated?	☐	☐	☐
c. give a speech in front of many people?	☐	☐	☐

Afterwards the class determines if men and women answer differently.

Give Your Opinion

This section helps students learn how to politely agree or disagree with someone in English. Students hear opinions on tape. A box to the side shows common responses, such as I think so, too, or I don't think so. For example, in Unit 6, "Fears and Phobias," students hear and respond to the following opinions:

Most teenagers are not afraid of anything.

Men try to hide their fears.

Intelligent people have more fears than other people.

Some fear is good.

Students are given an example and encouraged to add their own ideas. In supporting their opinions, students develop critical thinking skills.

Responses
I think so, too.
I don't think that's true.

Pronunciation Pointer

This part engages students in an activity to remedy a common pronunciation problem. After a short explanation and model, students do a task to show their understanding of the feature.
In Unit 1, for instance, students practice placing stress on content words when asking and answering *wh*-questions.

> **When** does it **leave**? It **leaves** at **noon**.
> **When** does it **arrive**? It **arrives** at **5 pm**.
> **How long** does it **take**? It **takes five hours**.
> **How much** does it **cost**? It **costs 300 dollars**.

Listening Comprehension 1 and 2

These sections include a variety of listening activities. In some, students supply missing words or phrases, in some they indicate comprehension, and in some they do tasks based on the listening.

The content is practical and interesting. For example, students hear airline announcements, marketing information, and "fun facts" stories. Again, the level of the language is controlled, though the content is geared to adults and young adults.

Conversation Practice

In this part, a variety of activities help students improve their conversation skills.
For example, in the Breakfast unit, after listening to a conversation in a restaurant, students look at a menu and practice ordering. In the Air Travel unit, they do an Information Gap in which they find out about different flights. In the Games and Sports unit, students do an Information Gap in which they learn where and when different Olympic Games were held. Some units provide students with social language (functions) that they practice in conversations. In other units there is a focus on new vocabuary, while in still others there is a discussion based on something they had previously heard or read.

Check This Out

A final piece of art—a cartoon, an advertisement, a puzzle, a painting—in combination with a short task gets students motivated once again to consider and talk about another aspect of the topic.

Acknowledgments

Students are the final arbiters of the value of a text. I thank my students at the International English Language Institute, Hunter College, CUNY, both for their helpful comments and for their enthusiastic reaction to the materials in *Topics from A to Z*.

I also thank Emily Wonson who came to observe my classes as part of her MA TESOL program, and ended up making valuable suggestions about some of the activities in this book.

Publishers are the ones who decide whether or not to use their resources to develop and produce a book. My thanks to all the people at Pearson Education who supported the concept of this series and helped bring it to fruition:

To Joanne Dresner, President of Pearson North America, who listened to my initial ideas for *Topics from A to Z*, and encouraged me to develop them.

To Ginny Blanford who first managed this project.

To Sherry Preiss and Laura Le Drean who offered many specific and valuable ways to improve the book and who were so supportive throughout.

To Robert Ruvo who diligently guided the book through production.

To Tara Maldonado for her photo research.

To my development editor, John Barnes who managed to cut, simplify, and modify materials in ways that always seemed obvious after he had done them, while answering all my queries with good humor and kindness.

To Debbie Sistino who took the book through the final editing stages and made sure that all the final details would be taken care of in time for production.

As always, my special thanks to my family—to Harris, Dan, and Dahlia for their love, support, and interest in my work.

Unit 1   Air Travel

When you are at an airport for a few hours, what do you do?

- Buy souvenirs?
- Watch TV?
- Call friends?
- Visit the duty free shop?
- Other?

Facts

A. GROUPS Try to complete the sentences.   **Were you right?**

1. A plane takes _____ and lands.   ___yes___

   a. up   b. away   c. off

2. You can travel first class, business class, or _____.   _____

   a. low class   b. coach   c. third class

3. After traveling a long distance in a plane, many people have jet _____.   _____

   a. lag   b. set   c. dreams

4. The world's busiest airport is _____.   _____

   a. Tokyo Narita   b. Paris Charles de Gaulle   c. Chicago O'Hare

5. The first flight attendants were single, female _____.   _____

   a. cooks   b. teachers   c. nurses

6. In 1987 American Airlines saved $40,000. The airline stopped putting _____   _____
   in each salad in first class.

   a. an olive   b. a tomato   c. a carrot

🎧 **Now listen and check your answers.**

B. GROUPS

- Take turns saying the facts. Then close your books.
- How many facts can you remember? Say all the facts you remember.

Talk about Your Experience

A. PAIRS Answer the questions. Then ask your partner. Add information.

    Example: A: *Do you like to travel?*
                   B: *Yes, I do. I love to see new places. Do you?*
                   A: *I used to, but now I don't.*

	YOU	YOUR PARTNER
• Do you like to travel?		
• How do you like to travel?		
• Have you traveled by plane? If so, where did you go? When? Why?		
• Are there things you don't like about air travel?		
• Do you ever get jet lag? What do you do about it?		

B. WHOLE CLASS Survey three students.

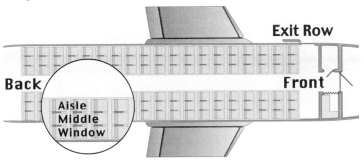

Where do you like to sit on a plane? Why?

Report the results to the class.

Example: *Two students like to sit in the front and on an aisle. One student doesn't care.*

Give Your Opinion

A. 🎧 Listen to these opinions.

B. PAIRS Take turns. Student A reads an opinion. Student B responds and adds information.

    Example: A: *Airline food is terrible.*
                   B: *I disagree. The meals on some airlines are good.*

Responses
I agree.
I disagree.

A. 🎧 Listen and repeat the questions and answers. Stress the words in bold print.

When does it **leave**? It **leaves** at **noon**.
When does it **arrive**? It **arrives** at **5 pm**.
How long does it **take**? It **takes five hours**.
How much does it **cost**? It **costs 300 dollars**.

B. PAIRS Take turns asking and answering the questions. Pay attention to the stressed words.

Listening Comprehension 1

🎧 Listen to the announcement at Vancouver Airport. Check the flights that were canceled or delayed because of bad weather.

Airline	Destination	Canceled	Delayed
Japan Airlines #15	Tokyo, Narita		
Air Canada #776	Honolulu		
United Airlines #845	Los Angeles		
Alaska Airlines #2285	Anchorage, Alaska		
Aeromexico #9312	Acapulco		
United Airlines #8624	New York, JFK		

Conversation Practice

Information Gap

PAIRS Student A turn to page 106. Student B turn to page 108.

PAIRS A man is buying a plane ticket. Listen to his conversation with a travel agent. Then answer the questions.

1. On what day of the week does the man first want to fly to Miami?

   _____.

2. When can he fly to Miami for $110?

   _____.

3. Does the man buy a ticket? Why or why not? _____.

Check This Out

GROUPS Read the cartoon. Then answer the questions.

Has your baggage ever gone to the wrong place?

Would you like to travel to the future? Why or why not?

Would you like to travel to the past? Why or why not?

Unit 2 — Breakfast

What do you do during breakfast?

tropical fruit

yogurt

miso soup

A. GROUPS Guess which statements are true (T) and which statements are false (F).

Your answer			Were you right?
_F_	1.	"Brunch" is a combination of breakfast and ~~dinner~~. *lunch*	_yes_
_____	2.	Many people in the U.S. and Canada eat "fast food" for breakfast.	_____
_____	3.	Espresso is weak coffee.	_____
_____	4.	When you "fast," you don't eat anything. The word "breakfast" comes from "breaking (ending) the fast" of the night.	_____
_____	5.	In many European countries, rice is a part of breakfast.	_____
_____	6.	In Brazil, people often have rice and miso soup as part of breakfast.	_____

🎧 **Now listen and check your answers. Change the false statements to true ones.**

B. GROUPS
- Take turns saying the facts. Then close your books.
- How many facts can you remember? Say all the facts you remember.

A. PAIRS Answer the questions. Then ask your partner. Add information.

Example: A: *Do you eat a big breakfast?*
B: *No, I just have a bowl of cereal. What about you?*
A: *I have a big breakfast. I eat cereal, eggs, and toast.*

	YOU	YOUR PARTNER
• Do you eat a big breakfast?		
• Do you eat breakfast alone?		
• Do you eat breakfast before 6 AM?		
• Do you drink two cups of coffee in the morning?		

Tell the class about your partner.
Example: *Pat eats a big breakfast, and she eats alone.*

B. WHOLE CLASS Survey five students. Choose three questions, or ask your own.

Do you ever...

skip (not eat) breakfast?
drink green tea in the morning?
eat fast food in the morning?
eat rice in the morning?

Report the results to the class.
Example: *I learned that two students skip breakfast.*
Three students never skip breakfast.

> **Reporting**
> I learned that...
> I found out that...

A. 🎧 Listen to these opinions.

Breakfast is the most important meal of the day.

It's important to have something hot for breakfast.

Coffee is healthier than tea.

If you want to lose weight, skip breakfast.

B. PAIRS Take turns. Student A reads an opinion. Student B responds and adds information.

Example: A: *It's important to have something hot for breakfast.*
B: *I don't think so. I never do.*
A: *What do you have?*
B: *Fruit, yogurt, bread, and cheese. And I drink milk.*

> **Responses**
> I think so, too.
> I don't think so.

A. 🎧 Listen to these questions. The voice always rises at the end of *yes/no* questions.

SERVER	CUSTOMER
Are you ready to order? or Ready to order?	Do you have any orange marmalade?
Would you like something to drink?	Do you have any hot cereal?
Do you want more coffee? or More coffee?	Do you have any green tea?
Is that all?	Do you have any juice?

B. PAIRS Take turns asking the questions. Be sure your voice rises at the end of each question.

Listening Comprehension 1

🎧 Listen to the conversation at a restaurant. Look at the breakfast menu. Mark the food and drinks that the people order. Write "M" for <u>man</u> and "W" for <u>woman</u>.

Breakfast Menu

Pancakes and Waffles			Beverages		
Three Pancakes	M	$5.00	Green Tea	____	$1.75
Two Waffles	____	$5.00	Herbal Tea	____	$2.00
			Coffee	____	$2.00
Eggs and Omelets			Decaf	____	$2.00
Two Eggs: fried, poached,			Milk	____	$1.75
or scrambled	____	$4.50			
Three-egg Omelet	____	$7.00	**Juices**		
			Apple	____	$2.50
Side Orders			Cranberry	____	$2.50
Bacon	____	$2.00	Grapefruit	____	$3.00
Sausage	____	$2.00	Orange	____	$3.00
Hash Browns	____	$1.25	Tomato	____	$2.50
Toast and Jelly	____	$1.25			

Conversation Practice

PAIRS Student A is a customer, and Student B is a server at a restaurant. Have a conversation. Use the menu above. Use *yes/no* questions, as in the Pronunciation Pointer above.

Example: Server: *Can I help you?*
                   Customer: *Yes, thank you. I'd like…*

A. 🎧 Read the chart. Listen to the results of an online survey about breakfast in Japan. Then listen again and complete the chart.

Online Survey–Breakfast in Japan 🇯🇵

1. What style breakfast do you eat?

Survey Results

a. Japanese style: 20%

b. Western style: _____

c. Western and Japanese: _____

d. _____: 13%

2. How much time do you spend eating breakfast?

Survey Results

a. 2-5 minutes: 6%

b. 5-10 minutes: _____

c. 10-15 minutes: _____

d. 15-20 minutes: 18%

e. over 20 minutes: _____

3. What do you usually drink for breakfast?

Survey Results

a. milk: _____

b. coffee: _____

c. _____ tea: 31%

d. English tea: _____

e. _____: 11%

4. What do you usually do while eating breakfast?

Survey Results

a. _____: 72%

b. read a newspaper: _____

c. _____: 23%

d. listen to the news on the radio: _____

e. listen to music: _____

B. WHOLE CLASS Now answer the questions. Then choose one of the questions above and ask five classmates. Write their answers on a sheet of paper.

Example: I talked to five students: 20% drink milk, 20% drink coffee, and 60% drink tea.

Check This Out

GROUPS

Is this the breakfast of the future?

Do you want to try this breakfast? Why or why not?

In 2002, silver was the most popular car color. What car color do you like?

Most Popular Car Color in 2002

North America	22%—silver	16%—white
Europe	40%—silver	19%—blue
Japan	19%—silver	19%—white

Facts

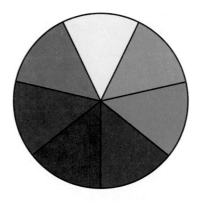

A. GROUPS Try to complete the sentences. Use the words below.

yellow	red	blue	green	white	purple

Were you right?

1. Brides wear _____ *red* _____ in traditional Chinese weddings. ___yes___

2. The three primary colors are red, blue, and _____. _____

3. A jealous person is _____ with envy. _____

4. When you're sad, you feel _____. _____

5. _____ is a combination of all colors. _____

6. If you combine red and blue, you get _____. _____

🎧 **Now listen and check your answers.**

B. GROUPS
- Take turns saying the facts. Then close your books.
- How many facts can you remember? Say all the facts you remember.

Talk about Your Experience

A. PAIRS Answer the questions. Then ask your partner. Add information.

Example: A: *What colors do you like to wear?*
B: *I like to wear black, beige, and white. How about you?*

	YOU	YOUR PARTNER
• What colors do you like to wear?		
• What colors do you almost never wear?		
• What colors are the walls in your home?		

B. WHOLE CLASS Tell the class about your partner's choice of colors. Then talk about the colors of your classroom. Do you like them? Do you want to change them?

Give Your Opinion

A. 🎧 Listen to these opinions.

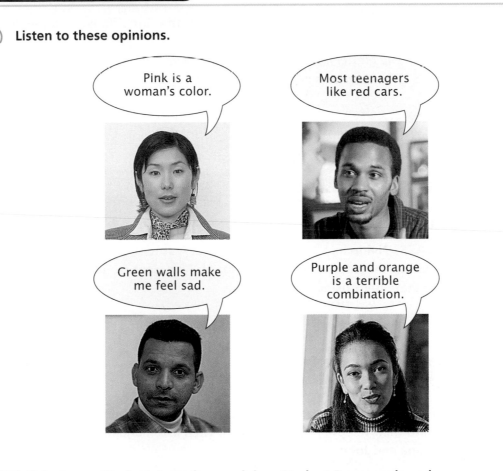

Pink is a woman's color.

Most teenagers like red cars.

Green walls make me feel sad.

Purple and orange is a terrible combination.

B. PAIRS Take turns. Student A reads an opinion. Student B responds and adds information.

Example: A: *Pink is a woman's color.*
B: *Really? I don't think so. I think both men and women can wear pink.*

Responses
Really? I think . . .
That's true.

A. **Listen to these sentences. What is the speaker correcting? Check the correct answer.**

1. The Canadian flag is red and **white**.
   - ☐ a. a mistake about the color
   - ☐ b. a mistake about the country

2. The **Canadian** flag is red and white.
   - ☐ a. a mistake about the color
   - ☐ b. a mistake about the country

Canada

Mexico

United States of America

In the first sentence the stress is on "white." The speaker is correcting someone who thinks the flag is another color.

In the second sentence the stress is on "Canadian." The speaker is correcting someone who thinks it's the flag of another country.

B. PAIRS Take turns making false statements about the three flags. Your partner will use stress to correct you.

Example: A: *The Mexican flag is red, white, and blue.*
                 B: *The **American** flag is red, white, and blue.*

In English, stress on a word can change the meaning of a sentence. We say the stressed word louder, longer, and at a higher pitch.

Conversation Practice

A. GROUPS Name three countries and the colors of their flags. Write this information on the board.

B. WHOLE CLASS Divide into two teams, A and B. A student from team A says a true or false statement about the information on the board. A student from team B says, "That's true," or corrects the statement using intonation.

Example: A: *The Brazilian flag is blue, green, and red.*
                 B: *No, that's wrong. The Brazilian flag is blue, green, and **yellow**.*

Listening Comprehension 1

John and Helena work for the same company, but in different countries. They've never met. Listen to their telephone conversation. Then listen again, and complete the descriptions of Helena and John.

	Hair Color	Eye Color	Color of Clothes
Helena			
John			

Warm up: Do you eat any blue food? What food?

A. 🎧 **PAIRS** Listen to a talk about color and food. Read the statements. Then listen again, and mark the items true (T) or false (F). Change false statements to true ones.

                                        candy

    __F__   1. M&M's is the name of an American ~~soda~~.

    _____   2. There are blue M&M's.

    _____   3. Many foods arc blue.

    _____   4. Blue is rare in nature.

    _____   5. Years ago people learned that blue, purple, and red were often signs of bad food.

    _____   6. When you want to sell food, taste is the only important thing.

B. **GROUPS** Are there foods that you don't eat because you don't like the way they look? Explain.

GROUPS Choose a favorite color. Then read what it says below about people who like that color. Is it true about you?

blue	red	green	purple	black	brown	gray	yellow

1. Blue: You enjoy a peaceful environment.
2. Red: You are energetic.
3. Green: You are easy-going.
4. Purple: You have unusual tastes.
5. Black: You prefer natural things.
6. Brown: You like the outdoors.
7. Gray: You'll try anything once.
8. Yellow: You like art.

Days, Months, and Numbers

About how many phone numbers do you know by heart (without checking)?

Average Number of Phone Numbers People Know By Heart	
Men	10
Women	9

Facts

A. GROUPS Try to complete the sentences.

Were you right?

1. A decade is _____ years.

   a. ten   b. one hundred   c. one thousand   _____

2. A century is _____ years.

   a. ten   b. one hundred   c. one thousand   _____

3. In Japan, Korea, and China, the number _____ is considered unlucky.

   a. three   b. four   c. thirteen   _____

4. When a baby is born in Korea, it is one _____ old.

   a. day   b. month   c. year   _____

5. People in most countries read the date 3/6 as June 3. In other countries they read it as _____.

   a. March 3   b. March 6   c. June 6   _____

6. Chinese New Year is sometimes in January and sometimes in February. It is based on _____.

   a. a lunar calendar   b. a solar calendar   c. the stars   _____

 Now listen and check your answers.

B. GROUPS

- Take turns saying the facts. Then close your books.
- How many facts can you remember? Say all the facts you remember.

Talk about Your Experience

A. PAIRS Answer the questions. Then ask your partner. Add Information.

> **Example:** A: *What's your favorite day of the week?*
> B: *I like Saturday best. I don't have to get up early. I usually go out Saturday night. What about you? What's your favorite day?*
> A: *Sunday. I play soccer every Sunday. It's my favorite sport.*

	YOU	YOUR PARTNER
• What's your favorite day of the week? Why?		
• What's your favorite season (spring, summer, fall, winter)? Why?		
• Do you have a lucky or an unlucky number? If so, what is it?		

How many classmates have a lucky or unlucky number? Are any of the numbers the same?

B. WHOLE CLASS Survey five students. Ask, "What's your favorite time of day? Morning? Afternoon? Evening? Night?"

	#1	#2	#3	#4	#5
Name					
Time of Day					

Report to the class.

> **Example:** *Kaori likes the morning. Carolina likes the evening. Hee Sook, Samuel, and Boris like the night.*

Give Your Opinion

A. 🎧 Listen to these opinions.

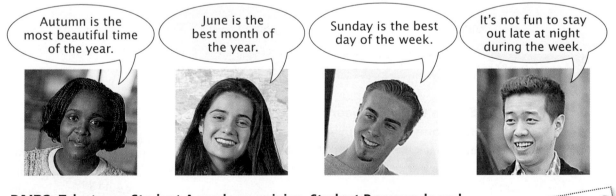

> Autumn is the most beautiful time of the year.

> June is the best month of the year.

> Sunday is the best day of the week.

> It's not fun to stay out late at night during the week.

B. PAIRS Take turns. Student A reads an opinion. Student B responds and adds information.

> **Example:** A: *Autumn is the most beautiful time of the year.*
> B: *That's not always true. Last year, it was really cold, and it rained all the time.*

Responses
That's true.
That's not always true.

NOTE	EXAMPLES
A syllable is a word or part of a word with one vowel sound.	One syllable: day Two syllables: Mon•day Three syllables: Sep•tem•ber Four syllables: un•im•por•tant Five syllables: co•in•ci•den•tal

A. 🎧 **Listen to the days of the week.**

All the days of the week have two syllables except for one day. Which day is that?

_____

B. 🎧 **PAIRS Listen to the months of the year. List them by syllables.**

One Syllable	Two Syllables	Three Syllables	Four Syllables
			January

C. PAIRS Take turns saying the days of the week and the months of the year.

Listening Comprehension 1

🎧 **Listen to the conversation. Then write the phone number and the address.**

Phone number: __ __ __ - __ __ __ - __ __ __ __

Address: _____ Street

Conversation Practice

A. GROUPS Take turns. Ask your classmates for important phone numbers in your area.
Example: What's the number of the police?

B. GROUPS Take turns. Now ask your classmates for important addresses in your area.
Example: What's the address of our school?

> **Responses**
> **Asking for and Giving Clarification**
> Could you say it more slowly?
> What was that again?
> Let me say it again.
> Excuse me?
> Let me repeat that.

Warm up: Imagine that three people in your class have the same birthday. Are you surprised?

A. 🎧 **PAIRS** When things happen together in a surprising way, we call it a coincidence. Listen to this talk about coincidences. Then read the sentences. Listen again and complete the sentences.

President
John F. Kennedy

President
Álvaro Obregón

Coincidences

1. The names Kennedy and Obregón have _____ each.

2. Both men were assassinated. Their assassins had _____.

3. Both assassins died _____ killing the president.

4. Both Kennedy and Obregón were married in years ending in _____.

5. Both Kennedy and Obregón had a son who _____ soon after birth.

6. Both men came from _____.

7. Both men died in their _____.

B. **WHOLE CLASS** Tell about a coincidence in your life.

Check This Out

GROUPS Do you like math puzzles? Why or why not?

PAIRS Look at the calendar. Ask a partner to choose any four dates that make a square (for example: 9, 10, 16, 17). Ask your partner to tell you the SUM of the numbers (in this example, 52), but NOT the numbers.

Can you find the four numbers? Can you explain how to do this? (The solution is on page 107.)

JANUARY 2005

Sunday	Monday	Tuesday	Wednesday	Thursday	Friday	Saturday
						1
2	3	4	5	6	7	8
9	10	11	12	13	14	15
16	17	18	19	20	21	22
23	24	25	26	27	28	29
30	31					

How often do you check your e-mail?

Checking e-mail

WELCOME
You Have E-Mail

76 %
Daily

23%
Weekly

1%
Less than
once a week

Facts

A. GROUPS Try to complete the sentences. Use the words below.

electronic	address	online	snail	laptop	by the way

Were you right?

1. Today we talk about two types of mail, e-mail and _____ mail.   _____

2. A _____ is a computer you can carry with you.   _____

3. The letters BTW in an e-mail message mean _____.   _____

4. The "e" in e-mail stands for _____.   _____

5. Your personal e-mail location is called your e-mail _____.   _____

6. When you are connected to the Internet, you are _____.   _____

🎧 Now listen and check your answers.

B. GROUPS
- Take turns saying the facts. Then close your books.
- How many facts can you remember? Say all the facts you remember.

Talk about Your Experience

A. PAIRS Answer the questions. Then ask your partner. Add information.

Example: A: *Do you use a computer?*

B: *Yes, I do. Do you?*

A: *Occasionally. I don't have a computer, and I don't need one.*

	YOU	YOUR PARTNER

• Do you use a computer?
• What do you use it for?
  • to send and receive e-mail?
  • to shop?
  • to do research?
  • to read the news and weather reports?
  • to play games?
  . to meet people?
• If you don't use a computer, why not?		

B. WHOLE CLASS Survey three students. Ask the following questions:

1. What do you use a computer for most often?
2. What is one reason you like computers?
3. What is one reason you don't like computers?

Report the results to the class.

Example: *Two students use a computer for e-mail.*

One student uses a computer for research.

Give Your Opinion

A. 🎧 Listen to these opinions.

The Internet is a great way to meet people.

Computers are the greatest invention of the 20th century.

A lot of information on the Internet isn't true.

The Internet has made the world smaller.

B. PAIRS Take turns. Student A reads an opinion. Student B responds and adds information.

Example: A: *The Internet is a great way to meet people.*

B: *I don't agree. In my opinion, there are a lot of crazy people. It's dangerous to meet people on the Internet.*

Responses
You're right.
I don't agree. In my opinion, . . .

Pronunciation Pointer /i/ and /ɪ/

A. Listen to the sound of /i/. It is a long, tense vowel sound.

I rec<u>ei</u>ve twenty <u>e</u>-mail messages a day.
Don't l<u>ea</u>ve your s<u>ea</u>t.

Listen again and repeat the sentences. Smile when you say /i/.

B. Listen to the sound of /ɪ/. It is a short, relaxed vowel sound.

Can you f<u>i</u>x <u>i</u>t?
<u>I</u>f she qu<u>i</u>ts, I qu<u>i</u>t.

Listen again and repeat the sentences.

C. Listen to /i/ and /ɪ/. Repeat the words.

s<u>ea</u>t   s<u>i</u>t   h<u>ea</u>t   h<u>i</u>t   p<u>ee</u>l   p<u>i</u>ll

D. **PAIRS** Listen. Circle the sentence you hear. Then say a sentence to your partner. Your partner decides which sentence you said and says *A* or *B*.

	A	B
1.	Don't slip.	Don't sleep.
2.	Hit it now.	Heat it now.
3.	Fill this glass.	Feel this glass.
4.	Look at the ship.	Look at the sheep.

Listening Comprehension 1

When something goes wrong with a computer, we say, "There's a bug in the computer." Listen to a conversation about that expression. Then answer the questions. Give the man's answers for 1–4.

1. When was the word "bug" first used for a computer problem? In _____.

2. Where was the word first used? At _____.

3. Who solved the problem? _____.

4. What kind of bug caused the problem? A _____.

5. Is Sam correct? _____.

Conversation Practice — Words with Two Meanings

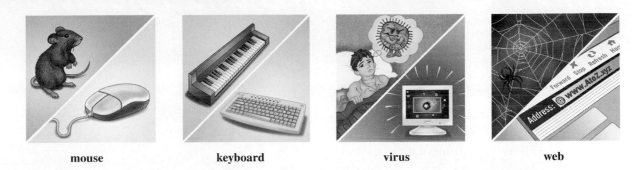

| mouse | keyboard | virus | web |

A. PAIRS Each pair of pictures above shows a computer-related meaning for a word and a meaning that is not about computers. Write one sentence for each of the words.

B. WHOLE CLASS Read each of your sentences to the class. The class decides if:
a. the sentence is about a computer.
b. the sentence is not about a computer.
c. the sentence may be about a computer.

Examples: *Where's the keyboard? (c)*
She plays keyboard and he sings. (b)
Where are the numbers on your keyboard? (a)

Listening Comprehension 2

Warm up: Many people read about health and medical problems on the Internet. Is that a good idea? Why or why not?

 A reporter is asking people on the street about the Internet. Listen and answer the questions.

1. What is the man's occupation?

   _____.

2. What does the man like about the Internet?

   _____.

3. What does the man dislike about the Internet?

   _____.

Check This Out

GROUPS Discuss these questions.
Do you get more e-mail or regular mail?
Do you get too much mail?

"*You've got mail.*"

What other things are people afraid of?

Biggest Fears: Online Survey	
Speaking in front of a big audience	32%
Looking down from a tall building	28%
Flying in planes	11%
Standing in crowds	8%
Other	21%

Facts

A. GROUPS Try to complete the sentences.

<u>Were you right?</u>

1. To fear something is to be _____ of it.

    a. proud   b. aware   c. afraid   _____

2. When you're very scared, you might say, "I'm scared to _____.

    a. death   b. pieces   c. my heart   _____

3. An actor is nervous before a play. He has _____.

    a. stage fright   b. stage fear   c. stage care   _____

4. Someone is nervous before an event. She says, "I have

    _____ in my stomach."   _____

    a. birds   b. butterflies   c. bees

5. Phobias are strong fears of things that are not really dangerous.

    Phobias, such as a fear of flying are more common in _____.   _____

    a. men   b. women   c. older people

6. Social phobias, such as a fear of meeting new people, are _____.   _____

    a. more common   b. more common   c. equally common in
        in women   in men   men and women

     **Now listen and check your answers.**

B. GROUPS
- Take turns saying the facts. Then close your books.
- How many facts can you remember? Say all the facts you remember.

Talk about Your Experience

A. PAIRS Answer the questions. Then ask your partner. Add information.

Example: A: *As a child, did you have any special fears?*
   B: *Yeah, I was afraid of spiders. How about you?*
   A: *I was really afraid of big dogs.*

	YOU	YOUR PARTNER

• As a child, did you have any special fears (for example, a fear of the dark)?
• When did you stop being afraid?
• When you are afraid, what happens to your body?
  • Does your heart beat fast?
  • Do you sweat?
  • Do you scream?		

B. WHOLE CLASS Survey five students. Ask the questions below. On a separate piece of paper, keep a record of the answers and whether they are from men or women.

Is it easy for you to: **Yes**   **No**   **Sometimes**

a. start a conversation with someone you've just met?   ☐   ☐   ☐

b. enter a room when most people are seated?   ☐   ☐   ☐

c. give a speech in front of many people?   ☐   ☐   ☐

Report the results to the class.

C. WHOLE CLASS Compare the answers of men and women to the questions in Part **B**. Are there differences between them?

Example: *Two men said it was hard to give a speech in front of many people, but no women said that.*

Give Your Opinion

A. 🎧 Listen to these opinions.

Most teenagers are not afraid of anything.

Men try to hide their fears.

Intelligent people have more fears than other people.

Some fear is good.

B. PAIRS Take turns. Student A reads an opinion. Student B responds and adds information.

Example: A: *Most teenagers are not afraid of anything.*
   B: *I don't think that's true. Many teenagers are afraid of not being liked.*

Responses
I think so, too.
I don't think that's true

A. 🎧 **Listen to these conversations. Note the stress on** *too* **and** *either*.

1. A: I'm afraid of mice.
   B: I am, **too**.

2. A: He's not afraid of snakes.
   B: I'm not, **either**.

3. A: We're afraid of spiders.
   B: They are, **too**.

4. A: She's not afraid of cockroaches.
   B: We're not, **either**.

B. PAIRS Now practice reading the conversations with a partner. Remember to stress *too* and *either*.

C. PAIRS Complete each sentence in two ways. Your partner agrees or disagrees. Don't forget to stress *too* and *either*.

I'm afraid of _____. I'm not afraid of _____.

Example: A: *I'm afraid of mice.*
   B: *I am, too.*

   A: *I'm not afraid of cockroaches.*
   B: *I'm not, either.*

Listening Comprehension 1

🎧 **GROUPS** Listen to the conversation. Which sport is the person trying to learn? Why do you think so?

American football	water skiing	diving	in-line skating	sky diving

WHOLE CLASS Compare your answers with other groups. (The answer is on page 107.)

Conversation Practice   Overcoming a Fear

Jill had a fear of elevators. This happened after she got stuck in an elevator for four hours. After that, Jill always walked up and down the stairs. She told people she needed the exercise.

Then, Jill got a great new job. The job was on a high floor in a tall building. She rode the elevator with her boss. They talked during the ride and she forgot her fear. She took the elevator again, and again she talked during the ride. After a while, she didn't feel afraid. She was very happy to overcome her fear.

PAIRS Have you ever overcome a fear? If so, what was the fear? Tell your partner what happened.

🎧 **Read the letter below. Then listen to an answer to the letter. Answer the questions.**

Dear Frieda,

Last month my Dad got a great job and we moved to this town. Our new home is beautiful and everyone in my family is happy except me. I'm really sad here. I don't have any friends and I'm afraid to meet anyone. Everyone in this high school is beautiful and smart. I don't belong here.

Sad & lonely

1. What advice does Frieda give Sad & Lonely?
2. Is her advice good?
3. Do you have any other suggestions?

Check This Out

These are phobias of famous people.

This is Andre Agassi, a famous tennis player. Reportedly, he is afraid of spiders.

This is Billy Bob Thornton, a famous actor. Reportedly, he has a fear of old furniture.

GROUPS

Do you know anyone with a phobia? What is it?

Games and Sports

List your five favorite sports or games. Rank them from 1 to 5.

MOST POPULAR SPORTS IN CANADA		
	Men	Women
#1	Golf	Swimming
#2	Hockey (ice)	Golf
#3	Baseball	Baseball
#4	Basketball	Volleyball
#5	Volleyball	Skiing (downhill)

Facts

A. GROUPS Try to complete the sentences.   **Were you right?**

1. Golf began in _____.   _____

   a. Japan   b. the United States   c. Scotland

2. A "good sport," _____.   _____

   a. is very athletic   b. doesn't get angry   c. runs fast
                            about losing

3. The Olympics began in _____.   _____

   a. Greece   b. Italy   c. Brazil

4. A marathon is a race of about _____   _____

   a. 13 miles   b. 12 miles   c. 26 miles

5. "Love" means no points in _____.   _____

   a. marriage   b. life   c. tennis

6. A king, a queen, and a knight are part of a _____ game.   _____

   a. checkers   b. chess   c. backgammon

🎧 **Now listen and check your answers.**

B. GROUPS
- Take turns saying the facts. Then close your books.
- How many facts can you remember? Say all the facts you remember.

Talk about Your Experience

A. PAIRS Answer the questions. Then ask your partner.

Example: A: *Do you play any sports?*
                B: *No, I don't. Do you?*
                A: *Yes, I do. I play golf. It's my favorite sport.*

	YOU	YOUR PARTNER
• Do you play any sports? Which ones? If not, why not?		
• Do you watch sports on TV? Which ones? If not, why not?		
• Do you like to watch the Olympics on TV? What sports do you like to watch? If you don't, why not?		
• Do you play computer games? Cards? Board games? Chess?		

B. WHOLE CLASS Discuss these questions.

Do you have a favorite team? What team?
Do you like a particular athlete? Who? Where is he or she from? Why do you like this athlete?
Do you have a favorite game? What game?

Give Your Opinion

A. 🎧 **Listen to these opinions.**

Sports are important for teenagers.

Boxing is too violent.

Winning is everything.

Computer games are good for the brain.

B. PAIRS Take turns. Student A reads an opinion. Student B responds and adds information.

Example: A: *Sports are important for teenagers.*
                B: *It depends. Some teens love sports, and some teenagers have other interests.*

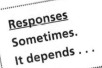

Responses
Sometimes.
It depends . . .

Pronunciation Pointer   *Thirteen or thirty?*

Some numbers in English are easy to confuse, for example, *thirteen* and *thirty*.

A. 🎧 **Listen to the stress of these numbers. It's always on the first syllable.**

30 40 50 60 70 80 90

B. 🎧 **Listen again and repeat. Pay special attention to the stress.**

C. 🎧 **Listen to the stress of these numbers. It can vary.**

13 14 15 16 17 18 19

D. 🎧 **Listen again and repeat. Pay special attention to the stress.**

Listening Comprehension 1

 Listen to these facts about the Olympics. Complete the sentences with the correct numbers.

1. The first modern Olympic Games took place in Athens, Greece in 1896.

   There were _____ people in the stadium.
              (17,000 / 70,000)

2. Olympic Games take place every four years, but in _____ and in _____
                                      (1916 / 1960)   (1914 / 1944)

   the Games were canceled due to war.

3. The first Winter Olympics were in 1924 in Chamonix, France. In _____, the
                                                            (1918 / 1980)

   _____ Winter Olympic Games took place in Lake Placid in the United States.
   (13th / 30th)

Conversation Practice   **Information Gap**

PAIRS Student A turn to page 106. Student B turn to page 108.

Listening Comprehension 2

Warm up: If you met Tiger Woods, what questions would you ask him?

Tiger Woods

🎧 **Listen to these questions and answers about Tiger Woods. Then complete the chart below.**

Tiger's real name: _____ Woods

Height: _____

Weight: _____

Date of birth: _____

Hometown: _____ , California

Education: 3 years at _____ University

Power color: _____

Check This Out

Mia Hamm

Serena Williams

Se Ri Pak

GROUPS

Do you think that athletes are paid too much money? Why or why not?

Holidays and Special Occasions

Were you ever in a parade?
On what occasion?
What did you wear?
What did you do?

Junkanoo is a holiday celebrated only in the Bahamas. There is a spectacular parade with music, dance, and costumes.

Facts

Carnaval

Chinese New Year

anniversary

graduation

A. GROUPS Guess which statements are true (T) and which statements are false (F).

Your answer		Were you right?
_____	1. Labor Day is a holiday for workers.	_____
_____	2. People celebrate their anniversary on the day they were born.	_____
_____	3. Ch'suk is an important holiday in Thailand. It's like the American Thanksgiving.	_____
_____	4. New Year's Eve is the night of New Year's Day.	_____
_____	5. Teacher's Day is not a holiday in the United States.	_____
_____	6. People get a bachelor's degree when they get a divorce.	_____
_____	7. In Brazil during Carnaval, people wear costumes and sing in the streets.	_____

🎧 **Now listen and check your answers. Change the false statements to true ones.**

B. GROUPS
- Take turns saying the facts. Then close your books.
- How many facts can you remember? Say all the facts you remember.

Talk about Your Experience

A. PAIRS Answer the questions. Then ask your partner. Add information.

Example: A: *What do you enjoy about holidays and special occasions?*
             B: *I enjoy seeing family and friends, and I enjoy inviting people to my home.*
                What about you?
             A: *I enjoy everything about holidays.*

	YOU	YOUR PARTNER
• What do you enjoy about holidays and special occasions?		
• What don't you enjoy about them?		
• getting and giving gifts		
• seeing your family and friends		
• not working or studying		
• eating special foods		
• wearing beautiful new clothes		
• inviting people to your home		

Tell the class about your partner.

Example: *Dan likes giving gifts, but he doesn't like wearing costumes or being in parades.*

B. WHOLE CLASS Tell the class about your favorite holiday. Give three reasons why it's your favorite.

Example: *My favorite holiday is Mother's Day. I like this day because I get to see my whole family. We have a delicious barbecue at my uncle's house. We give gifts to all the mothers. We play ball and have a good time.*

Give Your Opinion

A. 🎧 Listen to these opinions.

It's hard to choose good gifts.

I usually eat too much on holidays.

I love to send greeting cards on holidays.

Holidays are mainly for children.

B. PAIRS Take turns. Student A reads an opinion. Student B responds and adds information.

Example: A: *It's hard to choose good gifts.*
             B: *I don't think so. I think it's fun to choose gifts.*
                What do you think?
             A: *I think it's hard to choose gifts. I worry*
                that the person may not like my gift.

Responses
That's right.
I don't think so.

A. 🎧 Listen to these questions. Note the rising and falling intonation.

> Do they like fish or chicken?
>
> Should we buy her a CD or a video?
>
> Do you want to eat in or eat out?
>
> Should I get him a sweater or a shirt?

B. 🎧 Listen again and repeat. Pay special attention to the intonation.

C. PAIRS Ask a partner what he or she prefers. Pay special attention to the intonation.

Climate: warmer weather or colder weather
Food:　meat or fish
Music: classical or popular music
Sports: soccer or basketball
Games: computer games or board games

Example:　A: *Do you prefer warmer weather or colder weather?*
　　　　　　B: *I like warmer weather.*

Listening Comprehension 1

🎧 **Maria asks her friend, John, to help her choose a gift for her dad.
Listen to their conversation. Then complete the sentences.**

　1.　What does Maria decide to buy her father? She decides to buy a _____.

　2.　Does she decide to surprise him? _____.

Conversation Practice

PAIRS Take turns. Read each question aloud. Use the correct intonation. Guess the answers.

1.　Do you send a sick friend a "get well soon" card or a "sympathy card"? _____

2.　Is a prom a dance or a dinner? _____

3.　When a sixteen-year-old girl has a party in the U.S., is it called a "sweet sixteen" party or a "sweet
　　girl" party? _____

4.　Is a gift for a new home a "housewarming gift" or a "gift horse"? _____

🎧 **Listen and check your work. (The answers are on page 107.)**

Warm up: Do you ever feel stressed before holidays? Why?

A. 🎧 A psychologist says that holidays hold a "mixed bag" of feelings. People feel good and bad at holiday times. Listen to his advice about holidays. Check (✓) the advice he gives.

☐ 1. Decide what's most important for you.

☐ 2. Go away for holidays.

☐ 3. Give gift certificates.

☐ 4. Don't exchange gifts. Go to a show or restaurant instead.

☐ 5. Don't eat, drink, or party too much.

☐ 6. Stay within your budget.

B. **GROUPS** Dr. Ford gave several suggestions. Which ones do you agree with? Why?

Check This Out

Dogon male dancers

GROUPS

Do you wear special clothes on any holiday? What do you wear?

Ice Cream and Other Desserts

Do you like desserts better than the main course?

Facts

flan

tiramisu

tropical fruit

A. GROUPS Guess which statements are true (T) and which statements are false (F).

<u>Your answer</u>   <u>Were you right?</u>

_____ 1. People usually start a meal with dessert.   _____

_____ 2. Flan is a popular dessert in Spain and Mexico.   _____

_____ 3. Tiramisu is a popular dessert from Japan.   _____

_____ 4. 80% of the world's vanilla bean is grown in Madagascar.   _____

_____ 5. The most popular ice cream flavor in the United States is chocolate.   _____

_____ 6. In Brazil, desserts are often made with guava, avocado, mango,   _____
and coconut.

🎧 **Now listen and check your answers. Change the false statements to true ones.**

B. GROUPS
- Take turns saying the facts. Then close your books.
- How many facts can you remember? Say all the facts you remember.

Talk about Your Experience

A. PAIRS Answer the questions. Then ask your partner. Add information

Example: A: *Do you have a sweet tooth?*

B: *Yes, I do. I love to eat all sorts of sweet things —candy, ice cream, cookies, and cake. How about you?*

A: *I don't like sweets. I really don't like desserts.*

	YOU	YOUR PARTNER
• Someone with a "sweet tooth," likes to eat sweet things. Do you have a sweet tooth?		
• What's your favorite dessert?		
• How often do you eat ice cream (almost every day, often, sometimes, rarely, never)?		
• What's your favorite flavor? (vanilla, chocolate, etc.)		
• What dessert do you know how to prepare?		

B. WHOLE CLASS Shoppers in the U.S. prefer the following sweets: cookies, ice cream, frozen yogurt, doughnuts, ice milk/sherbet, pie, and cheesecake. Answer these questions:

Do you like any of these sweets? Which ones?
What sweets do shoppers in your country buy?

Give Your Opinion

A.  Listen to these opinions.

> I like desserts that look beautiful.

> Many desserts taste too sweet.

> Many desserts taste better with coffee.

> Fruit is the best dessert.

B. PAIRS Take turns. Student A reads an opinion. Student B responds and adds information .

Example: A: *I like desserts that look beautiful.*

B: *Really? I don't care how they look. I want my dessert to taste good.*

Responses
I agree.
Really?

A. 🎧 Listen to this children's rhyme. Which of the underlined words are stressed?

I scream, you scream,
we all scream
for ice cream.

B. Say the rhyme aloud.

C. 🎧 *Ice cream* is a compound noun; it is made of two separate words. In compound nouns, the stress is on the first word. Listen to these words and repeat.

| **ice** cream | **cheese** cake | **apple** pie | **rice** pudding | **chocolate** brownie |

D. **PAIRS** Tell your partner which of these desserts you like and don't like. Pay attention to stress.

Example: I like **ice** cream and **apple** pie. I don't like **cheese** cake, **rice** pudding, or **chocolate** brownies.

Listening Comprehension 1

🎧 Jan baked a chocolate cake. Listen to the conversation and circle the things that she put into the cake.

| sugar | cocoa | butter | water | baking soda | salt |
| (flour) | milk | oil | vinegar | vanilla | eggs |

Conversation Practice   Types of Food

PAIRS Add items to each category.

Junk Food (food with no health value)	Fast Food (food made and served quickly)	Snack (small amount of food eaten between meals)	Candy (sweet food made of sugar or chocolate)	Chip (thin dry piece of vegetable fried in oil)
soda	hamburger and fries	nuts	M&M's	potato chips

Talk with your partner. What do you eat? What don't you eat?

WHOLE CLASS Tell the class what you and your partner both like to eat.

Example: We both like chips, especially potato chips.

🎧 **Listen to these facts about ice cream. Then listen again and complete the statements.**

1. Ice cream was invented in _____ around _____ years ago.

2. The Roman Emperor Nero made a dessert with fruits and _____.

3. In 1812 Dolly Madison, the wife of an American President, served ice cream at an important ball. It was a big _____.

4. The ice cream cone was introduced in _____.

5. The top five consumers of ice cream are the United States, _____, Denmark, _____, and Belgium.

What do you think of these facts? Do any of them surprise you? Which ones?

Check This Out

PAIRS Do you prefer a beautiful dessert or a big dessert?

Unit 10 Jazz and Other Types of Music

**Do you like jazz?
Why or why not?**

Louis Armstrong and Ella Fitzgerald

Facts

A. GROUPS Try to complete the sentences.

Were you right?

1. Jazz started among _____.

   a. slaves from West Africa　　　b. farmers from Ireland　　　c. painters from Paris

   _____

2. A popular type of music in which the words are spoken, not sung, is called _____.

   a. tap　　　　　　　　b. rap　　　　　　　　c. zap

   _____

3. The leader of an orchestra is called a _____.

   a. boss　　　　　　　b. general　　　　　　c. conductor

   _____

4. When we hear something we like, we say, "That's music to my _____."

   a. heart　　　　　　b. ears　　　　　　c. head

   _____

5. The music of Bach, Beethoven, and Mozart is called _____ music.

   a. antique　　　　　b. traditional　　　　c. classical

   _____

6. Traditional music played by the ordinary people of an area is called _____ music.

   a. folk　　　　　　b. free　　　　　　c. fire

   _____

🎧 **Now listen and check your answers.**

B. GROUPS
- Take turns saying the facts. Then close your books.
- How many facts can you remember? Say all the facts you remember.

Talk about Your Experience

A. PAIRS Answer the questions. Then ask your partner. Add information.

Example: A: *What's your favorite kind of music?*
B: *I love jazz. I have over 50 jazz CDs. What about you?*
A: *I love all kinds of music —jazz, rock, classical, and folk.*

	YOU	YOUR PARTNER
• What's your favorite kind of music?		
• Who's your favorite musician?		
• Do you usually listen to music on the radio, on TV, on CDs, or at concerts?		
• Do you have a favorite music store?		
• Can you play an instrument? If so, which one?		
• When do you listen to music?		

B. WHOLE CLASS Tell the class how you and your partner are alike and different when it comes to music.

Example: *Marta likes rap music, but I don't. We both like folk music.*

Give Your Opinion

A. 🎧 Listen to these opinions.

CDs are too expensive.

Music brings people together.

It's hard for musicians to make money.

Karaoke is fun.

B. PAIRS Take turns. Student A reads an opinion. Student B responds and adds information.

Example: A: *Karaoke is fun.*
B: *I don't agree. I can't sing. I think it's boring.*

Responses
I agree.
I don't agree.

Spoken English has a special rhythm.

A. 🎧 **Listen to the rhythm of this conversation, first with words and then with "da-da-DAs."**

A: Listen to this.	da-da-da-DA
B: Who's singing?	DA-da-da
A: Maria Carey.	da-DA-da-DA-da
A: Isn't she incredible?	dadaDAdaDAdada
B: She sure is.	daDAda

B. PAIRS Take turns. Chant the rhythm before each sentence. Then say the sentence using the rhythm.

Example: *da-da-da-DA*   *A: Listen to this.*
               DA-da-da   *B: Who's singing?*
               da-DA-da-DA-da   *A: Maria Carey.*
               dadaDAdaDAdada   *Isn't she incredible?*
               daDAda   *B: She sure is.*

Listening Comprehension 1

GROUPS Try to complete these sentences.

1. This is a famous symphony by Beethoven. Some say it is the sound of your future knocking on the door. It's Beethoven's _____ Symphony.

2. This song was sung by the Beatles. The title is a past time word. The song is called _____.

3. Many young people in the United States sang this song in the 1960s. The name of the song is, "_____ Overcome."

4. At Princess Diana's funeral, Elton John sang, "_____ in the Wind."

5. This popular movie starring Sylvester Stallone is about a boxer. The name of the boxer and the movie is _____.

🎧 **Listen and check your answers.**

PAIRS Many people listen to music while doing other things. Do you? Complete the chart. Then ask your partner what kind of music he or she listens to. Answer your partner's questions.

SITUATION	YOU	YOUR PARTNER
• You're driving.		
• You're studying.		
• You're exercising.		
• You're eating dinner.		
• You're on an elevator.		
• You're in the shower.		

Example: A: *What kind of music do you like to listen to when you're driving?*
  B: *It depends. Sometimes I listen to rock, and sometimes I listen to rap. What about you?*
  A: *I usually listen to jazz. But sometimes I don't listen to music. I listen to the news.*

Listening Comprehension 2

Warm up: What do you know about Brazilian music? Do you know the song, "The Girl from Ipanema"? If so, do you like it? Why or why not?

Listen to a talk about Brazilian music. Choose a phrase from the right to complete the sentences on the left. Write the letter on the line.

1. Jazz and Brazilian music _____.
2. Astrud Gilberto _____.
3. Stan Getz and Charlie Byrd _____.
4. Joao Gilberto and Carlos Jobim _____.

a. developed the Bossa Nova
b. are American musicians
c. sang "The Girl from Ipanema"
d. have African roots

Check This Out

Born in northeastern Brazil, Astrud Gilberto is called "the Queen of Bossa Nova." She is a singer, songwriter, and artist.

WHOLE CLASS Do you know a song with English words? Tell the class about the singer and composer. Bring a CD or cassette to class, and play the song.

Astrud Gilberto

Kangaroos, Koalas, and Australia

This is the Sydney Opera House. Some say it looks like a sailboat. Others say it looks like a folded napkin. What does it look like to you? Do you like it? Why or why not?

Sydney Opera House

Facts

Great Barrier Reef

kangaroo

koala

Crocodile Dundee

A. GROUPS Try to complete the sentences.

Were you right?

1. The capital of Australia is _____.
   a. Melbourne   b. Canberra   c. Sydney   _____

2. The Great Barrier Reef is the largest _____ in the world.
   a. coral structure   b. bridge   c. island   _____

3. Koalas are related to _____.
   a. pandas   b. bears   c. kangaroos   _____

4. Baby kangaroos and baby koala bears travel in their mother's _____.
   a. pocket book   b. purse   c. pouch   _____

5. Koalas eat mostly the leaves of the _____.
   a. palm tree   b. eucalyptus tree   c. maple tree   _____

6. Baby kangaroos are called _____.
   a. joeys   b. kittens   c. puppies   _____

7. Paul Hogan starred in the Australian movie called _____.
   a. *Crocodile Dundee*   b. *Romancing the Stone*   c. *Bend it Like Beckham*   _____

   🎧 **Now listen and check your answers.**

B. GROUPS
• Take turns saying the facts. Then close your books.
• How many facts can you remember? Say all the facts you remember.

Talk about Your Experience

A. PAIRS Answer the questions. Then ask your partner. Add information.

Example: A: *Have you been to Australia?*
B: *No, I haven't.*
A: *Would you like to go there?*
B: *Yes. I'd love to go there. I'd really like to see the Great Barrier Reef.*
My friends tell me the fish there are incredible.

	YOU	YOUR PARTNER
• Have you been to Australia? If so, when? What did you see?		
• If not, would you like to go there? Why or why not?		
• What would you like to do in Australia? • snorkel on the Great Barrier Reef • hike in the outback (away from cities and towns) • visit Sydney • swim at the beach • see Australian animals in a zoo		

B. WHOLE CLASS Survey five students. Ask the following questions:

1. When someone speaks about Australia, what do you think of? Kangaroos and koalas? The Sydney Opera House? Crocodile Dundee? Native Australian art? Nicole Kidman and Paul Hogan? The 2000 Olympics?

2. Have you seen any Australian films? What do you remember about them?

Give Your Opinion

A. Listen to these opinions.

B. GROUPS Take turns. Read an opinion. Each student responds and adds information.

Example: A: *Nothing exciting happens in Australia.*
B: *Really? I think you can do many exciting things in Australia. You can hike, snorkel, and see all sorts of interesting sights.*
C: *I agree with B. I'd love to spend a month in Australia.*

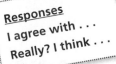

Responses
I agree with . . .
Really? I think . . .

Pronunciation Pointer   *Can* and *Can't*

A. When *can* is followed by a verb, we usually reduce the vowel sound in *can*. We stress the verb that follows.

I can **fly** tonight.

When *can't* is followed by a verb, we don't reduce the vowel sound in *can't*. We stress both *can't* and the verb.

I **can't fly** tomorrow.

B. Listen and repeat these sentences. Pay attention to stress and the reduced vowel sound in *can*.

I **can't understand** you.
He can **understand** me.
We can **go** to the beach tomorrow.
We **can't go** to the zoo on Sunday.
She can **help** us.
They **can't wait**.

C. PAIRS Complete the sentences with *can* or *can't*. Take turns reading your sentences aloud. Your partner then writes your sentences.

1. I _____ understand them.
2. We _____ see you later.
3. You _____ tell him.
4. She _____ speak Indonesian.

Check your partner's sentences.

Listening Comprehension 1

The Sydney Opera House isn't just an opera house. There are other things you can do there. Listen to the conversation. Then complete the sentences with *can* or *can't*.

1. You _____ eat there.
2. You _____ watch sports events.
3. You _____ see dance performances.
4. You _____ see plays.
5. You _____ see movies.
6. You _____ hear jazz and pop music.
7. You _____ hear talks.
8. You _____ play soccer.

Conversation Practice

A. Three of the sentences below are incorrect. Listen and change them. Then work with a partner. Take turns saying the sentences. Pay special attention to the pronunciation of *can* and *can't*.

1. A kangaroo can hop 60 kilometers per hour (40 miles per hour).
2. A kangaroo can weigh up to 85 kilograms (187 pounds).
3. A kangaroo can walk or move backwards.
4. A kangaroo can live with very little water.
5. Most kangaroos can move their legs one at a time.

B. PAIRS Do you know any interesting facts about other animals? Tell your partner.

Warm up: Look at the picture. Then look at the chart below. Can you complete any part of the chart?

Uluru

Former name of Uluru: _____

Important to native Australians for _____ reasons

Located: In _____ Territory of Australia

Distance around rock: _____

Distance to top of rock: _____

Shape of rock: _____

Most beautiful times to look at rock: _____

Year name changed to Uluru: _____

🎧 **Listen and complete the chart.**

Check This Out

GROUPS Rock art shows the presence of people in Australia for at least 30,000 years.

Is there any rock art in your country?

In what other parts of the world can you find rock art?

What do you think of this art?

Australian Rock Art

Unit 12   Love

Some say love is blind. Do you agree?

"I don't care if she is a tape dispenser. I love her."

© The New Yorker Collection 1998 Sam Gross
from cartoonbank.com. All Rights Reserved

Facts

A. GROUPS Try to complete the sentences.

Were you right?

1. On Valentine's Day in Japan, _____ chocolates.   _____
   a. women give men   b. men give women   c. men and women
                                                                 give their sweethearts

2. A romantic idea is often not _____.   _____
   a. good   b. loving   c. practical

3. A matchmaker introduces people for the purpose of _____.   _____
   a. arranging marriages   b. lighting fires   c. matching blood

4. When a man asks a woman to marry him, he often says, _____.   _____
   a. "Do you want to marry me?"   b. "Will you marry me?"   c. "Could you marry me?"

5. A blind date is a date with a person _____.   _____
   a. you have never met before   b. who cannot see   c. who wears funny clothes

6. People _____ in love.   _____
   a. call   b. crawl   c. fall

7. A person who disappoints you in love breaks your _____.   _____
   a. brain   b. heart   c. liver

🎧 **Now listen and check your answers.**

B. GROUPS
- Take turns saying the facts. Then close your books.
- How many facts can you remember? Say all the facts you remember.

Talk about Your Experience

A. PAIRS Answer the questions. Then ask your partner. Add information.

Example: A: *How romantic are you?*
B: *Not very. I prefer good food and large portions to a beautiful place with flowers. How about you?*
A: *Me? I'm just the opposite. I like flowers and candlelight dinners.*

	YOU	YOUR PARTNER

• How romantic are you?
  • I'm very romantic.
  • I'm a bit romantic.
  • I'm more practical than romantic.
  • I'm practical. I'm not romantic.
• Is love more important than money?
• Can you love more than one person at the same time?		

B. WHOLE CLASS Do a survey: How romantic are your classmates?

Example: *Five students are very romantic. Four are a bit romantic. One is not romantic.*

What's romantic to you?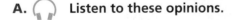
  • a candlelight dinner
  • a walk on a beach
  • a walk in the rain
  • an expensive piece of jewelry
  • a poem
  • other _____

Give Your Opinion

A. 🎧 Listen to these opinions.

Everyone needs romance.

Romance and marriage don't go together.

You need time to be romantic.

Romance is more important today than in my parents' time.

B. GROUPS Take turns. Read an opinion. Each student responds and adds information.

Example: A: *Everyone needs romance.*
B: *That's right. It's what makes life great.*
C: *I'm not sure about that. I think you can have a great life without romance. Romance only lasts a short time.*

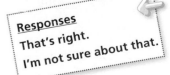

Responses
That's right.
I'm not sure about that.

A. 🎧 Listen to these tongue twisters. When we pronounce /l/, the tongue touches the part of the mouth just behind the upper teeth. When we pronounce /r/, the tongue does not touch anything.

Lilly looks like a little girl in that lacey lilac suit.
Randy reads romances while Ronnie runs in the rain.

PAIRS Practice the tongue twisters with a partner. Say them three times. Try to say them faster each time.

B. 🎧 Listen and repeat these words.

| liver—river | lake—rake | correct—collect | glow—grow | Ilene—Irene | lice—rice |

C. 🎧 Now listen and circle SAME or DIFFERENT.

1. SAME	DIFFERENT	4. SAME	DIFFERENT
2. SAME	DIFFERENT	5. SAME	DIFFERENT
3. SAME	DIFFERENT	6. SAME	DIFFERENT

Listening Comprehension 1

🎧 Listen to the phone call from Lilly to her friend Rita. Then look at the pictures. Circle Lilly's cousin, Ron.

Conversation Practice

PAIRS Name three good friends. Your partner will ask about them. Answer your partner's questions.

<u>Asking About People</u>
What's he or she like?
What does he or she do?
What does he or she like to do for fun?

Clara is a radio talk show psychologist. Listen to this letter from a listener. Then answer the questions.

1. What does Jennifer do?

   _____

2. What does Mike do?

   _____

3. What did Mike ask Jennifer to do?

   _____

4. Why is she upset?

   _____

GROUPS What do you think of Mike's request? What advice would you give Jennifer?

Check This Out

GROUPS A red or pink heart is the symbol of love. Make up a new symbol of love.

WHOLE CLASS Show your group's symbol to the class and explain it.

Unit 13 Movies

Do you prefer to watch movies at home or at a movie theater? Why?

Facts

A. GROUPS Guess which statements are true (T) and which statements are false (F).

Your answer		Were you right?
	star	
_____	1. The person with the main role in a movie is the ~~sun~~ of the movie.	_____
_____	2. *Titanic* was a popular movie about an airplane crash.	_____
_____	3. When a film's words are spoken in another language, we say the movie is dubbed.	_____
_____	4. Steven Spielberg and Akira Kurosawa are actors.	_____
_____	5. India makes more films than any other country.	_____
_____	6. Very popular movies are called "blockbusters."	_____

🎧 **Now listen and check your answers. Change the false statements to true ones.**

B. GROUPS
- Take turns saying the facts. Then close your books.
- How many facts can you remember? Say all the facts you remember.

Talk about Your Experience

A. PAIRS Answer the questions. Then ask your partner. Add information.

Example: A: *How often do you go to the movies?*
B: *Three times a week.*
A: *You're kidding! That's a lot.*
B: *I know. I love movies.*

	YOU	YOUR PARTNER
• How often do you go to the movies? • What kind of movies do you enjoy most? • comedies • love stories • action films • drama • horror films • animated films		

B. WHOLE CLASS Tell the class in which ways you and your partner are alike.

Example: *Neither of us likes animated films. We both like action films.*

C. WHOLE CLASS Name three actors you like. Name three films you like. Ask five classmates about the actors and films.

Do you know _____? Do you like him (her)? Why or why not?
(name an actor)

Have you seen _____? Did you like it? Why or why not?
(name a film)

Give Your Opinion

A. 🎧 Listen to these opinions.

I like old movies.

I usually don't enjoy blockbusters.

I get angry when people talk during a movie.

It's good to cry at sad movies.*

B. PAIRS Take turns. Student A reads an opinion. Student B responds and adds information.

Example: A: *I like old movies.*
B: *I do, too. Do you know* Star Wars?
I've seen it at least twenty-five times.

Responses
Agreeing
I do, too. / I don't, either.
I agree*
Disagreeing
I don't. / I do.
I disagree*

A. Listen to these sounds and their meanings.

Mmm   (Something tastes good.)
Hmm   (Let me think about it.)
Uh-huh (Yes.)
Uh-uh   (No.)
Uh-oh   (Something is wrong.)

B. **PAIRS** Listen and repeat this conversation.

1. A: Would you like to see that movie tonight at 10:00?
   B: Uh-huh. Let's meet at the theater at 9:55.
   A: Hmm. That's late. Could we meet at 9:45?
   B: Sure. No problem.

2. A: Try some of this popcorn.
   B: Mmm. It's delicious. . . (*coughs*)
   A: Are you okay?
   B: Uh-huh. I just needed a drink.

3. A: Do you have the tickets?
   B: Uh-uh. I gave them to you.
   A: Uh-oh. I can't find them.

Conversation Practice

PAIRS Take turns saying the sentences below. Your partner responds with one of the sounds in parentheses.

1. A: Do you like popcorn?

   B: _____. (uh-huh / uh-uh)

2. A: Have some chocolate.

   B: _____. It's good. (mmm / hmm)

3. A: I lost my English dictionary.

   B: _____. (uh-oh / uh-uh)

Listening Comprehension 1

Listen to the conversation. Then fill in the blanks with the type of movie.

science fiction	drama	comedy	action

1. *Ma* is a / an _____.

2. *War Games* is a / an _____ film.

3. *Always Together* is a / an _____.

4. *Star Trek 10* is a / an _____ film.

Warm up: Do you watch old movies? Are there any you watch again and again? If so, which ones?

🎧 **Listen to "Video Tips" on *AZ Radio News Program*. Then check (✓) the correct movie.**

	Central Station	Shall We Dance?
This movie takes place in Brazil.	✓	
This movie takes place in Japan.		
This movie was made in 1998.		
This movie was made in 1996.		
This movie shows ballroom dancing.		
This movie is about a middle-aged man.		
This movie is about a woman and a boy.		

Check This Out

GROUPS Do you think movies are getting better, are the same, or are they getting worse?

Today's Movies
Getting better 45%
Getting worse 43%
Don't know 12%

Do you ever read newspapers from different countries? Which papers? Which countries?

EL GRAN DIARIO DE MEXICO

EL UNIVERSAL

Facts

A. GROUPS Guess which statements are true(T) and which statements are false(F).

Your answer		Were you right?
_____	1. The headline (the title of a newspaper story) gives the least important news.	_____
_____	2. A journalist writes reports for newspapers, magazines, or television.	_____
_____	3. Newspapers depend on advertising.	_____
_____	4. Editorials give opinions, not facts.	_____
_____	5. Local news tells the news of the world.	_____
_____	6. There are fewer ads in newspapers because of the Internet.	_____

 Now listen and check your answers. Change the false statements to true ones.

B. GROUPS
- Take turns saying the facts. Then close your books.
- How many facts can you remember? Say all the facts you remember.

A. PAIRS Answer the questions. Then ask your partner. Add information.

Example: A: *How do you get the news?*
   B: *I usually watch the news on TV. I also read the paper and sometimes I read the news on the Internet. How about you?*
   A: *I read the paper.*

	YOU	YOUR PARTNER
• How do you get the news? from TV? newspapers? the Internet? • What do you like to read (or hear)? • international news • local news • sports • business • entertainment —TV, movies, plays • editorials • advice column • other: _____ • What's in the news now?		

B. WHOLE CLASS Write the names of two popular newspapers in your area. Find out how many students read each paper. Which newspaper do most of the students read?

Newspaper	Students Who Read this Paper

Give Your Opinion

A. 🎧 Listen to these opinions.

Newspapers don't always tell the truth.

TV news is the most interesting.

The Internet gives the most up-to-date news.

In fifty years there won't be any newspapers.

B. GROUPS Take turns. Read an opinion. Each student responds and adds information.

Example: A: *Newspapers don't always tell the truth.*
   B: *You can say that again. Newspapers tell only one side.*
   C: *I really don't think so. Some newspapers tell both sides. They only give their opinion in the editorials.*

Responses
Strong Agreement
and Disagreement
You can say that again.
I really don't think so.

A. Listen and repeat these words.

/dʒ/: judge   join   pages   largest   package   age

/tʃ/: chair   child   nature   future   watch   lunch

B. Now listen to these sentences. Write /dʒ/ or /tʃ/ above the sounds in the underlined words.

[ ]   [ ]   [ ]   [ ]   [ ]
1. General George Chambers will visit children in Chester Hospital tomorrow morning.

[ ]   [ ]   [ ]   [ ]
2. There will be a jazz concert at the Charles Joyce Library on June 1.

[ ]   [ ]
3. The fire in Bloom's caused damage to much of the store.

[ ]   [ ]   [ ]
4. The governor is changing the Chinese language program in all high schools.

C. PAIRS Take turns reading the sentences.

Listening Comprehension 1

Listen to a conversation about the word *news*. Then complete the sentences.

1. The first speaker asks, "Is *news* the plural of the word _____.
2. The second speaker thinks that *news* comes from the first letters of _____, _____, _____, and _____.
3. The third speaker looks it up and explains that *news* comes from a _____ word.

Conversation Practice

A. PAIRS With your partner, decide on two important items in the news. Write them down.

_____

_____

B. WHOLE CLASS Read your sentences to the class. Did other groups write about the same events?

🎧 **Listen to this radio news broadcast. Listen again and check (✓) the correct information.**

1. The weather will be

   ☐ a. 45 degrees, sunny, a little windy.

   ☐ b. 54 degrees, sunny, a little cloudy.

   ☐ c. 45 degrees, sunny, a little cold.

2. The UN announces

   ☐ a. the Year of the Teen.

   ☐ b. the Year of Human Rights.

   ☐ c. the Year of Peace.

3. The President's speech is at State College

   ☐ a. this morning.

   ☐ b. this afternoon.

   ☐ c. tomorrow.

4. The street fair will be

   ☐ a. Sunday from 2 to 6.

   ☐ b. Saturday from 2 to 6.

   ☐ c. Sunday from 10 to 6.

Check This Out

Tony Blair today suggested that he ould not seek another referen n the EU constitu jected

treaty EU gai

"But I think you will understand why I ulate on losing it at

Berlin Wall Comes Down

Russia Sends Earth Satellite into Space

their sa

ple make their uey make their decision."

He stressed: "If the Britis no in this referendum, tha is then verdict. That is absolutely clear."

Murdoch's papers would withdraw support without a plebiscite.

This would appear to unambiguously reject a second vote uther referendums - although everal reporters at the hour long

Acknowledging the threat to his premiership if the British people rejected his recommend

Mandela Elected President

ster faced a barrage of questions about the European constitution

PAIRS What do you know about these events?

Do you know about these beaches? Which would you like to go to? Why?

Some of the World's Best Beaches
Anse Source d'Argent, Seychelles
Ipanema Beach, Brazil
Larvotte Beach, Monaco
Maroma, Mexico
Poipu Beach, Hawaii, U.S.
Surfers Paradise Beach, Australia

Facts

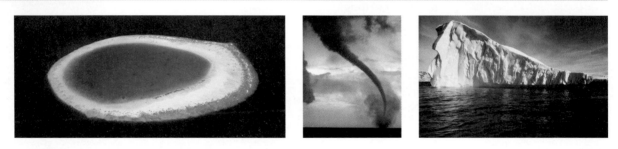

A. GROUPS Try to complete the sentences.   **Were you right?**

1. Oceans cover about _____ percent of the Earth's surface.   _____
   a. 50   b. 60   c. 70

2. There are_____ oceans on Earth.   _____
   a. four   b. five   c. six

3. The _____ Ocean is the largest ocean.   _____
   a. Atlantic   b. Pacific   c. Southern

4. Seas are smaller than oceans. The largest sea is the _____.   _____
   a. South China Sea   b. Mediterranean Sea   c. Red Sea

5. *Jaws* is a movie about a _____.   _____
   a. whale   b. dolphin   c. shark

6. *Moby Dick* is a book about a _____.   _____
   a. whale   b. dolphin   c. shark

7. At the beach people use _____ to prevent sunburn.   _____
   a. sunscreen   b. sunflower   c. sunset

🎧 **Now listen and check your answers.**

B. GROUPS
- Take turns saying the facts. Then close your books.
- How many facts can you remember? Say all the facts you remember.

Talk about Your Experience

A. PAIRS Answer the questions. Then ask your partner. Add information.

> **Example:** A: *What do you like to do at the beach?*
> B: *I like to swim or sit in the sun. What about you?*
> A: *I love to surf the waves.*

	YOU	YOUR PARTNER

• What do you like to do at the beach?
 	
  • swim
 	
  • surf the waves
 	
  • sit in the sun
 	
  • water-ski
 	
  • build castles in the sand
 	
  • fish
 	
  • other: _____		

B. WHOLE CLASS Tell about a beach you know. What color is the sand? What color is the ocean? Is the sand fine or coarse? Are there seashells? Are there palm trees? What do you like about this beach? Are there things you don't like about it?

Give Your Opinion

A. 🎧 Listen to these opinions.

Walking in the sand is good exercise.

Swimming in the ocean is better than swimming in a pool.

Looking at fish is relaxing.

Eating at the beach is fun.

B. GROUPS Take turns. Read an opinion. Each student responds and adds information.

> **Example:** A: *Walking in the sand is good exercise.*
> B: *Really? I don't think so. I like to exercise at the gym.*
> C: *I think both are good ways to exercise.*

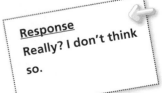

Response
Really? I don't think so.

A. 🎧 Listen to the /ou/ sound in the underlined letters. Repeat after the speakers.

> A: The <u>o</u>cean is c<u>o</u>ld.
> B: I kn<u>ow</u>. I stuck my t<u>oe</u> in it.

B. 🎧 Listen to the /ɔ/ sound in the underlined letters. Repeat after the speakers.

> A: Look. I c<u>au</u>ght a fish.
> B: I s<u>aw</u> it. You <u>ou</u>ght to take a picture.

C. 🎧 Listen to the sentences. Circle the /ou/ sounds. Underline the /ɔ/ sounds.

1. We **bought** a **boat**.
2. I **saw** him **sew** the swimsuit.
3. She **called** to say the water is **cold**.

D. PAIRS Say one of the boldfaced words in Part C. Your partner points to the word. Then switch roles.

Listening Comprehension 1

🎧 Listen to the telephone conversation. Mark the answers true (T) or false (F).

_____ 1. Ali woke Bob.

_____ 2. Ali invites Bob to swim in the ocean.

_____ 3. The water in the ocean is cold.

_____ 4. Bob's uncle bought a boat.

_____ 5. Bob and Ali will meet at the big clock.

Conversation Practice
Word Game

A. PAIRS The words below name things in the picture. Fill in the missing letters to complete the puzzle. The circled letters make a new word.
HINT: The new word is a polite word.

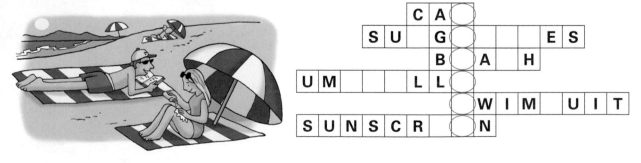

B. PAIRS Make up a story about the people in the picture. Who are they? Where are they? What are they going to do? What's going to happen?

C. WHOLE CLASS Tell your story to the class. The class votes on the best story.

Warm up: Does the sound of the ocean relax you?

🎧 **Listen to this relaxation tape. Then look at the pictures. Check (✓) the pictures that match the tape. Tell why the other pictures are incorrect.**

1. ☐

2. ☐

3. ☐

4. ☐

5. ☐

6. ☐

Check This Out

GROUPS This is a painting by the American painter, Winslow Homer. Does it go with the poem below? Why or why not?

> ### Sea Fever
>
> *(excerpt from a poem **Sea Fever** by John Masefield)*
>
> *I must go down to the sea again,*
> *to the lonely seas and the sky,*
> *And all I ask is a tall ship*
> *and a star to steer her by.*

High Cliff, Coast of Maine

Do you ever have "sea fever"?

Unit 16 · Parties

What do you think is the best place to meet new people of your age?

Places to meet

55% **Parties**

51% **Volunteer activities**

47% **Clubs**

A. GROUPS Try to complete the sentences. Use the words below.

| potluck | shower | anniversary | housewarming | bachelor | RSVP |

<u>Were you right?</u>

1. Sometimes before a man marries, his friends have a _____ party for him. _____

2. A party for a woman before she gets married is a bridal _____. _____

3. Everyone brings something to eat at a _____ party. _____

4. A party each year celebrating the day a couple got married is an _____ party. _____

5. A party for a new home is a _____ party. _____

6. _____ on an invitation means, "Please let me know if you can come." _____

Now listen and check your answers.

B. GROUPS
- Take turns saying the facts. Then close your books.
- How many facts can you remember? Say all the facts you remember.

Talk about Your Experience

A. PAIRS Answer the questions. Then ask your partner. Add information.

> *Example:* A: *What kind of parties do you enjoy?*
> B: *All kinds of parties. You name it. What about you?*
> A: *I like small parties. I guess I'm not much of a party person.*

	YOU	YOUR PARTNER
• What kind of parties do you enjoy?		
• Do you enjoy planning parties? Why or why not?		
• What's the hardest part about giving a party?		
• What's the hardest part about going to a party?		

B. WHOLE CLASS Do you usually have a birthday party? If not, do you do anything special on your birthday?

Describe a party you enjoyed. How many people were there? What was it for? What made the party fun for you?

Give Your Opinion

A. 🎧 Listen to these opinions.

> Big parties are more fun than small ones.

> I love surprise parties.

> You can't have a party without good food.

> I love to wear special clothes for a party.

B. PAIRS Take turns. Student A reads an opinion. Student B responds and adds information.

> *Example:* A: *Big parties are more fun than small ones.*
> B: *I'll say. I love a big party.*

> **Responses**
> Strong Agreement
> I'll say.
> Making a condition
> It depends.

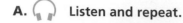
Linking words together makes your spoken English sound more natural. Look at the linked words.

A. 🎧 **Listen and repeat.**

1. A: There's a party on Saturday.
   B: What time is it?
   A: It's at 10 PM.
   B: Who's it for?
   A: It's for Andy.

2. A: There was a party for Mary.
   B: When was it?
   A: It was on the 20th at 8 PM
   B: Where was it?
   A: It was at Mario's Restaurant.

B. PAIRS Practice the conversations with a partner. Pay attention to the linked words.

Listening Comprehension 1

🎧 **Listen to Michelle's three phone messages. Write down the caller, the message, and the caller's phone number for each one.**

	Caller	Message	Phone number
#1			
#2			
#3			

Conversation Practice

Join Us!
For: Ginny Peters
When: June 23, 8 pm
Given by: Sherry Perry
Where: Bruno's Restaurant

Mr. and Mrs. Neil Wein
Mr. and Mrs. Joe Kane
Invite you to the marriage of their children

Heather and Mark

Saturday, the twenty-third   Maple Country Club
of June at nine o'clock   8 Sunset Drive
in the evening   Springfield, Connecticut

PAIRS Ask and answer questions about the invitations. One partner asks about
the birthday party; the other asks about the wedding.
Example: *Who's giving a party? When is it? Where is it? Who's it for?*

Warm up: When you're at a party with people you don't know, what do you talk to them about?

A. 🎧 **Listen to part of a conversation at a party. Fill in the blanks.**

1. A man starts a conversation with a woman. Complete the sentences.

   You look _____. Don't I _____ you _____ _____?"

2. How does she answer? _____.

   Do you think this is a good way to begin a conversation? Why or why not?

B. 🎧 **Now listen to the rest of the conversation and answer the questions.**

1. Where does the man work?
2. What kind of work does the woman do?
3. What does the man offer to bring the woman?
4. What does she ask for?

Check This Out

GROUPS Do you like to wear formal clothes?

Are formal clothes still popular today?

$800 million

1996

$1.4 billion

1998

Unit 17 — Quizzes, Tests, and Intelligence

Do you prefer to take paper tests or computer tests? Why?

"Keep your eyes on your own screen."

© The New Yorker Collection 1999 Barbara Smaller
from cartoonbank.com. All Rights Reserved.

Facts

A. GROUPS Try to complete the sentences. Use the words below.

pass	intelligence	copy	cram	quiz	choose

<u>**Were you right?**</u>

1. An IQ test measures _____ .   _____

2. When you _____ your classmate's answers, you are cheating.   _____

3. When you _____ for a test, you do all your studying just before the test.   _____

4. A short test is called a _____ .   _____

5. To succeed in a test is to _____ a test.   _____

6. A multiple-choice test lets you _____ from several possible answers.   _____

🎧 **Now listen and check your answers.**

B. GROUPS
- Take turns saying the facts. Then close your books.
- How many facts can you remember? Say all the facts you remember.

Talk about Your Experience

A. PAIRS Answer the questions. Then ask your partner. Add information.

Example: A: *What kind of tests do you prefer?*
                 B: *I like oral tests. What about you?*
                 A: *I prefer essays. I don't like multiple-choice tests. They're often*
                    tricky and I can't show what I know.

	YOU	YOUR PARTNER

• What kind of tests do you prefer?
 	
  • essays
 	
  • multiple-choice tests
 	
  • oral tests
 	
  • take-home tests (tests you do at home)		

B. WHOLE CLASS Discuss the following questions.
1. Why do students cheat on tests?
2. Do you only study because of tests? Why or why not?
3. Why are tests bad? Why are they good?

Give Your Opinion

A. **Listen to these opinions.**

B. PAIRS Take turns. Student A reads an opinion. Student B responds and adds information.

Example: A: *Many short tests are better than one long one.*
                 B: *That's not always true. I think one long test is*
                    better. But I really don't like tests.
                    I prefer to write a paper.

Responses
That's true.
That's not always true.

Plural Endings /s/ /z/, and /ɪz/

A. 🎧 The plural endings –s and –es have three different sounds.
Listen to these examples:

| test   tests | exam   exams | quiz   quizzes |

Words like *tests* end in an /s/ sound, words like *exams* end in a /z/ sound,
and words like *quizzes* have an extra syllable—they end in an /ɪz/ sound.

B. 🎧 Listen to the words. Write them in the correct places in the chart.

/s/	/z/	/ɪz/

C. PAIRS Take turns saying the words in the chart. Pay special attention to the plural endings.

Listening Comprehension 1

🎧 **Listen to this TV quiz show. Then answer the questions.**

1. The capital of Kenya is _____.
2. _____ had the first ski-through McDonald's.
3. The first table tennis games were played at the Olympic Games in _____.
4. The Aswan Dam is located in _____.

Conversation Practice   Game: /ɪz/ Endings

A. PAIRS Answer the questions. Raise your hand when you finish. The first pair to answer all the questions correctly wins.

1. Red flowers with a sweet smell are called r___s___s.
2. International restaurants serve d___sh___s from all over the world.
3. Minute and second hands are part of some wa___ ___ ___es.
4. Governments collect money from citizens through t___x___s.
5. In courts, lawyers try to convince j___dg___ ___ that their clients are innocent.
6. The sheets of paper in books are the p___g___ ___.
7. You can ride these animals. They are ho___ ___es.

B. PAIRS Take turns reading the sentences above. Pay special attention to the plural endings.

Warm up: Some intelligent people don't do well on intelligence tests. Why is that?

🎧 **Listen to a talk about Howard Gardner and his ideas about intelligence. Then match the items in columns A and B.**

A	B
1. Howard Gardner _____	a. Varied kinds of intelligences
2. Multiple intelligences _____	b. Ability to understand other people
3. Spatial intelligence _____	c. Traditional measure of intelligence
4. Interpersonal intelligence _____	d. Harvard University professor
5. Language and mathematical intelligence _____	e. Ability to see in pictures

Check This Out

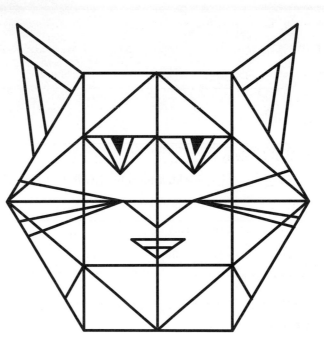

© ClassBrain, Inc. 2001; www.classbrain.com

GROUPS How many triangles are there? View the answer in a mirror: ɘɿutɔiq ꙅidt ni ꙅɘlǫnɒiɿt bɘɿbnud ɘno ylƚɔɒxɘ ɘɿɒ ɘɿɘʜT

1. This is a test of _____ intelligence.

   ☐ a. musical

   ☐ b. interpersonal

   ☐ c. spatial

Unit 18 Rain

Is there more news about good weather or bad weather? Why?

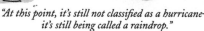

"At this point, it's still not classified as a hurricane—
it's still being called a raindrop."

DONNELLY

© The New Yorker Collection 2000 Liza Donnelly
from cartoonbank.com. All Rights Reserved.

Facts

A. GROUPS Try to complete the sentences.

Were you right?

1. People use a/an _____ to protect themselves from the rain.   _____

   a. bathing suit   b. umbrella   c. hairnet

2. The _____ is high before it rains.   _____

   a. humidity   b. community   c. river

3. A light rain is called a _____.   _____

   a. leak   b. hurricane   c. drizzle

4. After it rains, you can sometimes see a _____ in the sky.   _____

   a. rain date   b. rainbow   c. rain forest

5. Rain can form _____.   _____

   a. puddles   b. riddles   c. battles

6. Mount Wai-ale-ale in Hawaii has up to _____ rainy days a year.   _____

   a. 150   b. 250   c. 350

   Now listen and check your answers.

B. GROUPS

• Take turns saying the facts. Then close your books.

• How many facts can you remember? Say all the facts you remember.

Talk about Your Experience

A. PAIRS Answer the questions. Then ask your partner. Add information.

Example: A: *Have you ever lived in a very dry area?*

B: *Sure. Remember two years ago? There wasn't much rain here. We couldn't water the grass often, and we could only take showers every other day.*

	YOU	YOUR PARTNER
• Have you ever lived in a very dry area? What do people do to save water in very dry areas?		
• Have you ever lived in an area that gets a lot of rain? What do people do in areas with too much rain?		

• Can you remember a time when you _____ in the rain?
    • drove
    • played a sport
    • took a long walk
    • flew
    • went shopping		

• Tell about your experience.		

B. WHOLE CLASS What do you like about rain? What don't you like about rain?

Give Your Opinion

A. 🎧 Listen to these opinions.

It's fun to walk in the rain.

I rarely use an umbrella in the rain.

I don't like humid weather.

Everything seems cleaner after a long rainfall.

B. PAIRS Take turns. Student A reads an opinion. Student B responds and adds information.

Example: A: *It's fun to walk in the rain.*

B: *Do you think so? I usually stay indoors when it rains.*

Response
Do you think so?

🎧 **PAIRS** English places stress on different words in a sentence. Listen to these poems, called *limericks*. Practice them with your partner. Stress the words in bold print.

There **once** was a **man** from **Maine,**
Who **loved** to **walk** in the **rain.**
He **wore** wooden **shoes**
And **listened** to **blues,**
But **developed** big **blisters** and **pain.**

There was a young **man** from **Maine,**
Who **didn't have** much of a **brain.**
He **often** would **eat**
Spoiled **milk** and bad **meat,**
And **watered** his **plants** in the **rain.**

Listening Comprehension 1

🎧 Listen to the weather report. Then complete the chart. Use these words to describe the weather: *sunny, cloudy, rainy.*

	TEMPERATURE	WEATHER
Monday		
Tuesday		
Wednesday		

Conversation Practice
Information Gap

PAIRS Student A turn to page 106. Student B turn to page 108.

Warm up: Do you usually listen to the weather forecast? How often does the weather reporter make a mistake (usually, often, rarely, almost never)?

Listen to this talk about a weather reporter. Then mark the statements true (T) or false (F). Change the false statements to true ones.

_____ 1. Mike Lyons is a meteorologist.

_____ 2. He's on Eyewitness News 25.

_____ 3. He wants to change the weather.

_____ 4. Mike can make it rain.

_____ 5. Forecasters rarely make mistakes.

_____ 6. Native Americans pray for rain by having rain parties.

_____ 7. Native Americans are good forecasters because they understand geography.

Check This Out

Somewhere, over the rainbow, way up high,
There's a land that I heard of once in a lullaby.
Somewhere, over the rainbow, skies are blue,
And the dreams that you dare to dream really do come true.

GROUPS Read the beginning of the song "Somewhere Over the Rainbow." What does a rainbow mean to you?

Unit 19 — Sisters and Brothers

Are many older children unhappy when a new baby sister or brother arrives?

"*I hope you kept the box it came in.*"

© The New Yorker Collection 1999 Barbara Smaller
from cartoonbank.com. All Rights Reserved.

Facts

A. GROUPS Try to complete the sentences.

<u>Were you right?</u>

1. A _____ is one of two children who are born to the same mother at the same time. _____

   a. twin b. triplet c. half brother

2. A brother-in-law is the husband of your sister or the brother of your _____. _____

   a. husband b. son c. father

3. A person who doesn't have a sister or brother is called a/an _____ child. _____

   a. lonely b. single c. only

4. A "soul sister" is a term used for someone who _____. _____

   a. understands you b. sings with you c. likes jazz

5. A family _____ tells about the relationships in a family. _____

   a. flower b. tree c. plant

🎧 **Now listen and check your answers.**

B. GROUPS

- Take turns saying the facts. Then close your books.
- How many facts can you remember? Say all the facts you remember.

A. PAIRS Answer the questions. Then ask your partner. Add information.

Example:　A: *How many sisters and brothers do you have?*
　　　　　　B: *I have one older sister and two younger brothers. What about you?*
　　　　　　A: *I'm an only child. I don't have any sisters or brothers.*

	YOU	YOUR PARTNER
• How many sisters and brothers do you have?		
• Are you the oldest, youngest, middle, or only child in your family?		
• Is it better to be the oldest, youngest, or middle child? Why?		
• Are there any twins in your family? Do you know any twins? Are they identical (look exactly alike)?		

B. WHOLE CLASS What are the advantages and disadvantages of a large family?

Give Your Opinion

A. 🎧 Listen to these opinions.

Only children are usually spoiled*.

It's hardest to be a middle child.

Parents usually expect more of their first child.

Large families are happier than small ones.

B. PAIRS Take turns. Student A reads an opinion. Student B responds and adds information.

Example:　A: *Only children are usually spoiled.**
　　　　　　B: *You can't be serious. I know a lot of only children. They're very nice and fun to be with.*

> **Responses**
> **Strong Agreement and Disagreement**
>
> You can say that again.
> You can't be serious.

*act badly and expect to get everything they want

Pronunciation Pointer — Reduction of *and*

A. 🎧 When *and* connects two words, we often pronounce the *and* as *n*. Listen and repeat.

My sister and I (My sister n I)
My friend and I (My friend n I)
My aunt and uncle (My aunt n uncle)

B. 🎧 **PAIRS** Choose a word from those below to complete each sentence. Listen and check your work. Then take turns. Read a sentence to your partner. Remember to pronounce the *and* like *n*.

father	games	goes	bread	beans	then

1. He's not serious. For him life is all fun and _____.
2. Please pass the _____ and butter. I'm hungry.
3. It's a _____ and son business.
4. In Ecuador we ate a lot of rice and _____.
5. Now and _____ we visit Aunt Tilly.
6. He never stays in one place for long. He always comes and _____.

Listening Comprehension 1

GROUPS Do you know many only children? Are they all alike in any way?
Read these statements about only children. Check (✓) if you agree or disagree with them.

 Listen to a talk about only children. Check (✓) if the speaker agrees or disagrees with the statements.

	I agree	I disagree	The speaker agrees	The speaker disagrees
Only children are lonely.				
Only children don't play well with other children.				
Only children are self-centered.*				

* don't care about other people, only care about themselves.

A. Write five sentences about relatives.

    Examples: *My sister and I like to take long walks together.*
                      My brother and I argue about politics.
                      My mother and her sister talk on the phone every other day.
                      My father and his brother play golf together.

B. **PAIRS** Read your sentences. Your partner responds to each sentence with another sentence.

    Example: *A: My sister and I like to take long walks.*
               B: Really? My sister and I never take long walks. We talk a lot on the telephone.

Listening Comprehension 2

Warm up: These three English writers were also sisters. Do you know anything about them?

Ann Brontë

Charlotte Brontë

Emily Brontë

🎧 **Listen to a talk about the Brontë Sisters. Then complete the sentences.**

    1. They lived in the _____.

    2. The oldest sister was _____.

    3. Branwell was their _____.

    4. They liked to sit around _____.

    5. All of the sisters wrote _____.

    4. *Jane Eyre* was published in _____.

Check This Out

GROUPS In what fields are these brothers and sisters famous? Write the answers in the blanks. (The answers are on page 107.)

The Marx Brothers

Sunflowers

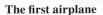
The first airplane

    _____ 1. Orville and Wilbur Wright   a. art

    _____ 2. Vincent and Theo Van Gogh   b. aviation (flying)

    _____ 3. The Marx Brothers   c. comedy films

Unit 20 — Telephones

Do you use a telephone more or less than you did five years ago? Why?

Telephone 60%
E-mail 34%
Letters 17%

How people communicate

Facts

A. GROUPS Guess which statements are true (T) and which statements are false (F).

Your answer			Were you right?
_____	1.	Alexander the Great invented the telephone.	_____
_____	2.	The first cell phones appeared in the 1970s.	_____
_____	3.	In the U.S., Europe, and Latin America, you can find business phone numbers in the Yellow Pages.	_____
_____	4.	An operation can help you make a call.	_____
_____	5.	When a phone is dead, you can't get a dial tone.	_____
_____	6.	"The line is busy" means someone is talking on the phone.	_____

🎧 Now listen and check your answers. Change the false statements to true ones.

B. GROUPS
- Take turns saying the facts. Then close your books.
- How many facts can you remember? Say all the facts you remember.

Talk about Your Experience

A. PAIRS Answer the questions. Then ask your partner. Add information.

Example: A: *Do you enjoy talking on the phone?*
B: *Not much. I make very few phone calls. I'd rather write to people or see them. How about you?*
A: *I love to talk on the phone. I think of a phone call as a visit.*

	YOU	YOUR PARTNER
• Do you enjoy talking on the phone? About how many calls do you make in a day (not more than two, three to five, five to ten, more than ten)?		
• Are most of your calls for business or pleasure?		
• Do you have an answering machine? Do you ever screen calls (listen to the machine before answering)? If so, when and why?		
• Do you have a cell phone? What is the best thing about a cell phone? What is the worst thing about one?		

B. WHOLE CLASS Do you think that women use the phone more than men? Why or why not?

Give Your Opinion

A. Listen to these opinions.

It's rude to use a cell phone in public*.

I don't like computer voices.

It's wrong for businesses to keep customers waiting on the phone.

It's dangerous to talk on the phone when you're driving.

B. GROUPS Take turns. Read an opinion. Each student responds and adds information.

Example: A: *It's rude to use a cell phone in public.*
B: *I agree with you. I only use a cell phone in public for very important calls.*
C: *Really? I use one all the time. I don't think it's rude unless I'm speaking in a loud voice.*

Responses

I agree with . . .

I disagree with . . .

*on a bus or train, at a performance, or in a restaurant

Pronunciation Pointer

/t/(ten), /θ/(three), and /ð/(the)

A. **Listen and repeat.**

That's the third wrong number today.
Take down these three names and telephone numbers.

B. PAIRS Some of these statements are incorrect. Read the statements. Say, "That's right" or "That's wrong." Change the wrong statements to correct ones. Take turns reading the correct sentences.

$1,121 + 1,212 = 3,303$

$4,590 + 5,432 = 10,022$

$3 \times 311 = 930$

The date between May 22nd and May 24th is May 25th.

The date after June 19th is June 20th.

Listening Comprehension 1

A couple is deciding on a message for an answering machine. Which message do they choose? Listen and check (✓) the correct answer.

_____ The longest message.

_____ The shortest message.

_____ The message that ends with "We'll get back to you soon."

GROUPS Do you agree with their choice? Why or why not?

Conversation Practice

A. PAIRS Write five short conversations. Use one of the sentences in the box for each conversation.

May I please speak to _____?

Please tell him I called.

Sorry. I must have called the wrong number.

Good talking to you.

Can I take a message?

Example: A: *May I please speak to Jonathan Lam?*
                    B: *Sorry. He isn't here right now.*

B. WHOLE CLASS Imagine all the telephones in your town stop working for the next 24 hours. You have no telephone or e-mail service. How would your life be different?

Example: A: *I usually call my friends and make plans to meet. I wouldn't be able to do that.*
B: *I need a phone for my work. I couldn't work.*
C: *My parents often call me. They might worry if the phone didn't work.*

Listening Comprehension 2

Warm up: Do you like simple phones or phones with many features? Why?

A. 🎧 **Listen to this ad for a picture phone. Check (✓) the features it offers.**

This phone:

- ☐ a. has a camera.
- ☐ b. comes in different colors.
- ☐ c. has a connection to the Internet.
- ☐ d. comes with a printer.
- ☐ e. is sold at all stores.

B. PAIRS Have you used such a phone? Would you like to? Why or why not?

Check This Out

GROUPS Can you think of a good reason to use a phone when someone is in the room with you?

"I have to hang up now. You just walked through the door."

Unit 21 — Urban and Rural Areas

Is your city on this list? Do you know the population of your city? Why is it hard to know how many people live in a big city?

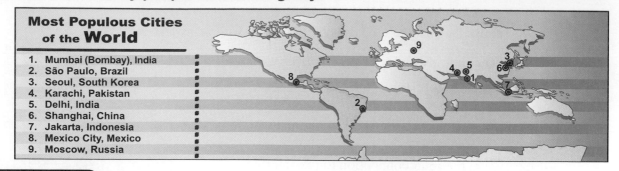

Most Populous Cities of the World

1. Mumbai (Bombay), India
2. São Paulo, Brazil
3. Seoul, South Korea
4. Karachi, Pakistan
5. Delhi, India
6. Shanghai, China
7. Jakarta, Indonesia
8. Mexico City, Mexico
9. Moscow, Russia

Facts

Trevi Fountain

Grand Palace

Taipei 101

A. GROUPS Try to complete the sentences.

<u>Were you right?</u>

1. Skyscrapers are _____.

   a. clouds   b. tall buildings   c. airplaines   _____

2. The tallest building in the world is in _____.

   a. Taipei   b. Prague   c. Tokyo   _____

3. The Tiber, the Han, and the Seine are _____ that divide cities.

   a. mountains   b. walls   c. rivers   _____

4. You can find the Grand Palace, floating markets, and a lot of traffic in _____.

   a. Taipei   b. Bangkok   c. Beijing   _____

5. The Trevi Fountain and the Coliseum are in _____.

   a. Florence   b. Venice   c. Rome   _____

6. Most people move from the countryside to the city for _____ reasons.

   a. social   b. economic   c. political   _____

🎧 Now listen and check your answers.

B. GROUPS

- Take turns saying the facts. Then close your books.
- How many facts can you remember? Say all the facts you remember.

Talk about Your Experience

A. PAIRS Answer the questions. Then ask your partner. Add information.

Example: A: *Where have you spent most of your life so far: in a city, the suburbs, or the countryside?*

B: *I lived in the countryside when I was a little boy. We moved to this city ten years ago. What about you?*

A: *I've always lived in a big city.*

	YOU	YOUR PARTNER
• Where have you spent most of your life so far: in a city, the suburbs (area around the city), or the countryside?		
• What is good and bad about life _____ ? ▪ in a big city ▪ in the suburbs ▪ in the countryside		
• What are three problems with the place you are in now?		

B. WHOLE CLASS What's important to you? Say something about each of the following:

stores	transportation	parks	entertainment	weather

Example: *I like music. I'd like to live near a music store. I like to take public transportation. I don't like to drive.*

Give Your Opinion

A. 🎧 Listen to these opinions.

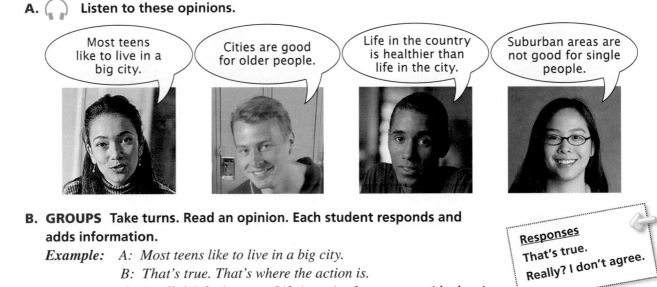

Most teens like to live in a big city.

Cities are good for older people.

Life in the country is healthier than life in the city.

Suburban areas are not good for single people.

B. GROUPS Take turns. Read an opinion. Each student responds and adds information.

Example: A: *Most teens like to live in a big city.*

B: *That's true. That's where the action is.*

C: *Really? I don't agree. Life is easier for teens outside the city.*

Responses
That's true.
Really? I don't agree.

Statements as Questions

Our voice goes up (rising intonation) when we want to ask a question. This happens even with statement word order.

A. 🎧 **Listen to these conversations. Then listen again and repeat the underlined sentences.**

A: You can stay with me.
B: <u>You're sure?</u>
A: I'm sure.

A: You can stay with him.
B: <u>He's in town?</u>
A: He's in town.

B. PAIRS Now practice the conversations with a partner. Switch roles.

C. 🎧 **Listen to these sentences. Circle STATEMENT or QUESTION.**

1. STATEMENT	QUESTION		5. STATEMENT	QUESTION
2. STATEMENT	QUESTION		6. STATEMENT	QUESTION
3. STATEMENT	QUESTION		7. STATEMENT	QUESTION
4. STATEMENT	QUESTION		8. STATEMENT	QUESTION

Listening Comprehension 1

🎧 **Look at three ads for apartments. The ads use the abbreviations listed below. Then listen to a conversation about an apartment. Circle the ad for the apartment that the woman is talking about.**

BR = bedroom
Ba = bathroom
LV = living room
DR = dining room
EIK = eat in kitchen

★Apartments★

* 3BR, 2Ba, LV DR, EIK

* 2BR, 3Ba, LV, DR, EIK, terrace

* 3BR, 2Ba, LV, EIK, terrace

Conversation Practice

A. PAIRS Which of these things would you like to have in your home? Rank them from 1 to 7 (1 = most important, 7 = least important).

a fireplace	a jacuzzi	a game room	a swimming pool
a ping-pong table		a tennis court	a sauna

What other luxuries would you like in your home?

B. WHOLE CLASS Tell the class what you learned about your partner's preferences.

Warm up: By 2050, two-thirds of the world's population will live in cities. There will be 54 mega cities, with more than 10 million people. At present there are 15. What will life be like in such mega cities?

🎧 **GROUPS** Listen to two people talk about life in the city and life in the country. Then write four more words they use to talk about the city and four more words they use to talk about the country.

Words that Describe Life in the City	Words that Describe Life in the Country
buildings	trees

Do you agree with the man or the woman? Why?

Check This Out

GROUPS Marc Chagall uses images from his childhood in the painting, *I and the Village* (1911). He gives a picture of village life. What would you put in a painting of your childhood?

Unit 22 Vacations

Who gets the most vacation days? Are you surprised? Why or why not?

Average Number of Vacation Days Each Year

Brazil	34	Italy	42
Canada	26	Japan	25
France	37	Korea	25
	USA	13	

Facts

A. GROUPS Try to complete the sentences.

Were you right?

1. In 2000 and 2001 the most popular place for tourists to visit was _____. _____

   a. France   b. India   c. Mexico City

2. According to the World Tourist Organization, in 2020 the most popular place for   _____

   tourists to visit will be _____.

   a. India   b. the U.S.   c. China

3. When people go camping, they sleep in _____. _____

   a. tents   b. motels   c. cabins

4. The newest Disney theme park outside the United States is in _____. _____

   a. Taipei   b. Hong Kong   c. Copenhagen

5. When you visit famous or interesting places, you are _____. _____

   a. sightseeing   b. sleepwalking   c. window shopping

6. A gift you buy to remember a vacation is called a _____. _____

   a. tour   b. guide   c. souvenir

   🎧 **Now listen and check your answers.**

B. GROUPS
- Take turns saying the facts. Then close your books.
- How many facts can you remember? Say all the facts you remember.

Talk about Your Experience

A. PAIRS Answer the questions. Then ask your partner. Add information.

Example: A: *What do you like to do on vacation?*
                B: *I like to visit a new place. When I'm at home, it doesn't feel like a vacation.*

	YOU	YOUR PARTNER

• What do you like to do on vacation?
  • relax at home
  • visit a new place
  • go to the beach or the mountains
  • spend time with friends or relatives
  • other: _____
 	
• How long do you think a vacation should be?
  • a week or less
  • two weeks
  • three weeks
  • four weeks
  • other: _____
 	
• Do you prefer one long vacation or several shorter ones?		

B. WHOLE CLASS Make a list of reasons why vacations are important.

Give Your Opinion

A. Listen to these opinions.

I think visiting a city is more interesting than visiting the countryside.

I don't like guided tours.

I like to buy souvenirs when I travel.

I don't like to travel.

B. PAIRS Take turns. Student A reads an opinion. Student B responds and adds information.

Example: A: *I don't like to travel.*
                B: *I don't either. I enjoy staying home with my friends.*

Responses
I do, too.
I don't, either.

Pronunciation Pointer /p/, /b/, /v/, and /f/

A. 🎧 **Listen and repeat these words.**

pet	bet	boat	vote
pit	bit	best	vest
fight	bite	fat	vat
fun	bun	fear	veer

B. 🎧 **Listen and circle the word you hear.**

1. pen   Ben
2. pear   bear
3. fun   bun
4. bet   vet
5. fan   van

6. four   bore
7. fit   bit
8. pan   ban
9. vine   fine
10. Pete   beat

C. 🎧 **Listen and repeat these sentences.**

Visit the very vibrant city of Venice.
Bryce Canyon is a beautiful place to be.
Florence has the finest art in Italy.
Pick a place to pitch the tent.

D. PAIRS Take turns repeating each sentence in Part **C** several times. Try to say it faster each time.

Listening Comprehension 1

🎧 Amy is going camping. Listen and check (✓) the things she has packed, the things she will pack, and the things she doesn't plan to take.

	Packed	Will Pack	Won't Take
a flashlight			
batteries			
a can of beans			
a box of matches			
a pillow			

Conversation Practice

A. GROUPS You're planning to go camping for three days. You can't take too many things. Take turns saying which of these things you will <u>not</u> take. Explain why.

1. a flashlight
2. batteries
3. a can of beans
4. a box of matches
5. a pillow

6. sunglasses
7. a watch
8. a book to read
9. a cell phone
10. a laptop

11. a walkman
12. a sleeping bag
13. a fishing rod

B. WHOLE CLASS Compare your list with other groups.

Bryce Canyon   Machu Picchu

A. 🎧 Listen to this ad for A to Z Tours to Bryce Canyon National Park in the USA, and Cuzco and Machu Picchu in Peru.

Listen again and fill in the blanks.

Bryce Canyon National Park

1. The tour begins in _____.

2. You will travel by _____.

3. You will stay at a _____.

4. You will see _____ formations.

5. You will learn about the _____ and _____ Americans.

Cuzco and Machu Picchu

1. The tour begins in _____.

2. You will stay in Cuzco for _____.

3. You can _____ the Inca Trail or ride the _____ to get to Machu Picchu.

Check This Out

GROUPS

Do you usually shop when you travel?

What do you buy?

About how much do you spend?

What people buy when they travel

Clothing or shoes 77%

Souvenirs 49%

Books or music 42%

Think of things people carry in their purse or pockets. Name one for each letter of the alphabet.

> **Examples:** A—aspirin
> B—book (small one)
> C—candy

How many letters could you find something for?

What's in a woman's purse?

$1 bill	75%
Gum/mints	59%
Tissues	57%
Lip balm	55%

Facts

Frida Kahlo

women voting

Queen Elizabeth II

Maria Sklodowska-Curie

A. GROUPS Try to complete the sentences.

Were you right?

1. A sister, an aunt, and a _____ are all female relatives. _____

   a. cousin   b. nephew   c. niece   d. son

2. All of the following are women except _____. _____

   a. a princess   b. a queen   c. a duchess   d. a prince

3. All of the following are famous women artists except _____. _____

   a. Frida Kahlo   b. Margaret Thatcher   c. Mary Cassatt   d. Georgia O'Keefe

4. Women in the U.S. won the right to vote in 1921. Women in Switzerland won the right to vote in _____. _____

   a. 1871   b. 1951   c. 1971   d. 1991

5. Women in New Zealand won the right to vote in _____. _____

   a. 1893   b. 1913   c. 1923   d. 1993

6. Ms. is the title for _____. _____

   a. married women only   b. unmarried women only   c. all women   d. men and women

🎧 **Now listen and check your answers.**

B. GROUPS
- Take turns saying the facts. Then close your books.
- How many facts can you remember? Say all the facts you remember.

Talk about Your Experience

A. PAIRS Answer the questions. Then ask your partner. Add information.

Example: A: *Who usually shops and cooks in your family?*
                 B: *My mom usually shops, but both my mom and dad cook. What about in your family?*
                 A: *My mom does the cooking. We all shop.*

	YOU	YOUR PARTNER

• Who usually does the following in your family, a man or a woman?
 	
  • shops
  • cooks
  • earns the money
  • takes care of the children
  • cleans the home
  • decides on vacations
  • plans weekends and holidays
  • fixes things in your home		

B. WHOLE CLASS Report to the class the differences between your family and your partner's family.

C. GROUPS Describe a woman you admire. (She doesn't have to be famous.)
Tell why you admire this person.

Example: *I admire my grandmother. My grandfather died young, and my grandmother raised five*
                 children. She taught them good values and gave them a good education.
                 Today they are all very successful and very close to her and to each other.

Give Your Opinion

A.   Listen to these opinions.

Women work harder than men.

Men are stronger than women.

Women are healthier than men.

Women are better bosses than men.

B. PAIRS Take turns. Student A reads an opinion. Student B responds and adds information.

Example: A: *Women work harder than men.*
                 B: *I'll say. Lots of women have jobs and do all*
                    the housework.

Responses
I'll say.
You can't be serious.

Irregular Plural Nouns

A. 🎧 These irregular plurals are often mispronounced. Listen and repeat.

| one man | two men | one child | two children |
| one woman | two women | one wife | two wives |

B. 🎧 Circle what you hear.

1. man   men
2. woman   women
3. child   children
4. wife   wives

C. PAIRS Take turns. Ask your partner questions. Begin with "How many". Use the phrases below.

men in class today / women in class today / children in your family / wives in class / men or women on a soccer team / men or women on a volleyball team

Example: *A: How many men are there in class today?*
             B: There are nine men. How many women are there in class today?

Listening Comprehension 1

Lisa A. Barron is a professor at the University of California's School of Management. She asked her students to roleplay a job interview. All her students applied for the same job. She discovered that the men asked for a higher salary (more money) than the women. She believes women need to learn how to ask for more money.

🎧 **Listen to her advice to women. Then read the statements below. Mark them true (T) or false (F). Change the false statements to true ones.**

Your answer		Were you right?
_____	1. Know the salary of the person who is interviewing you.	_____
_____	2. Before an interview, write down things you want from the job.	_____
_____	3. Tell your boss that salary is not important for you.	_____
_____	4. Get a good job title.	_____
_____	5. Don't talk about how you saved money at a job you had in the past.	_____

Listen again and check the six things she says to do.

Conversation Practice

Total Earnings of Full-Time, Year-Round Workers by Sex	Females	Males
Less than $10,000	4.4%	2.8%
$10,000 – $19,999	20.8%	12.3%
$20,000 – $24,999	13.9%	9.4%
$25,000 – $34,999	23.4%	19.1%
$35,000 – $49,999	20.0%	21.4%
$50,000 – $74,999	11.9%	19.2%
$75,000 and over	5.5%	15.8%

WHOLE CLASS Look at the chart on page 92. Write four statements. Read your statements to the class.

Examples: The largest percentage of men earn between $35,000 and $49,999 per year.
The largest percentage of women earn between $25,000 and $34,999 per year.

Listening Comprehension 2

Maya Angelou is a writer, poet, actor, songwriter, director, singer, and civil rights worker.

Listen to an excerpt from her poem
"Phenomenal Woman." Then listen again and
complete the lines.

Maya Angelou

Pretty women wonder _____
my secret lies,
I'm not _____ *or built to suit a*
fashion model's size.
But when I _____ *to tell them,*
They think I'm _____ *lies.*
I say,
It's in the reach of my arms,
The span of my hips,
The stride of my _____,
The curl of my _____,
I'm a woman.

phenomenal—very unusual and impressive
fashion model—someone whose job is to show clothes
span—the distance from one side to the other
the stride of my step—the way I walk

Check This Out

GROUPS When you look at this painting, do you think of the poem "Phenomenal Woman"? Why or why not?

Woman Powdering Herself, **Georges Seurat**

Look at this X-ray. What part of the body do you see?

(The answer is on page 107.)

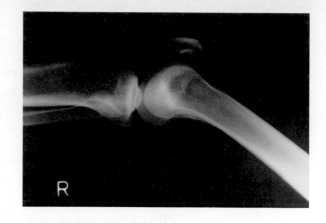

Facts

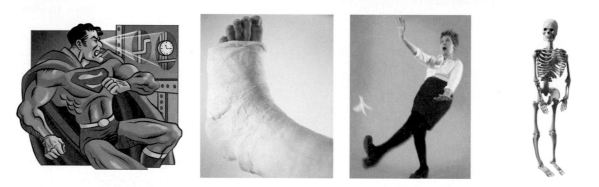

A. GROUPS Try to complete the sentences. Use the words below.

leg	cast	Roentgen	skeleton	Superman	accident

Were you right?

1. _____ discovered X-rays in 1895.   _____

2. The superhero with X-ray vision is _____.   _____

3. All the bones of the body together are the _____.   _____

4. To wish an actor good luck before a play, we say, "Break a _____."   _____

5. After you break an arm or leg, you usually wear a _____.   _____

6. When someone gets hurt without anyone meaning it to happen,
   we call it an _____.   _____

Now listen and check your answers.

B. GROUPS
- Take turns saying the facts. Then close your books.
- How many facts can you remember? Say all the facts you remember.

Talk about Your Experience

A. PAIRS Answer the questions. Then ask your partner. Add information.

Example: A: *Have you ever broken a bone?*
B: *Yes, I have. I broke my arm.*
A: *How did it happen?*
B: *I was skiing.*
A: *When was that?*
B: *Two years ago.*

	YOU	YOUR PARTNER
• Have you ever broken a bone? If so, how did it happen? When and where did it happen?		
• How do we know if a bone is broken?		
• Were you ever with a person who broke a bone? What did you do to help?		
• Have you ever helped an injured animal or bird?		
• Would you like to be a doctor, nurse, or other healthcare worker? Why or why not?		

B. WHOLE CLASS Survey five classmates.

Have you ever broken a bone?
What bone?
What were you doing when it happened?

Report the results to the class.

Example: *Juan broke his leg. He was playing soccer at the time. Maria broke a finger. She fell during a basketball game. Emiko, Victor, and Ali have never broken a bone.*

Give Your Opinion

A. Listen to these opinions.

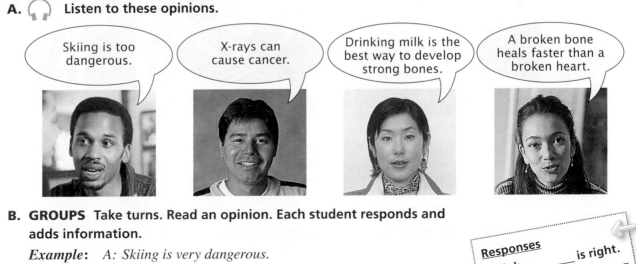

Skiing is too dangerous.

X-rays can cause cancer.

Drinking milk is the best way to develop strong bones.

A broken bone heals faster than a broken heart.

B. GROUPS Take turns. Read an opinion. Each student responds and adds information.

Example: A: *Skiing is very dangerous.*
B: *Really? I don't think so. All sports are dangerous.*
C: *I think A is right. There are always accidents at ski slopes, especially when the slopes are crowded.*

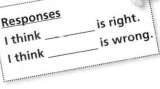

Responses
I think _____ is right.
I think _____ is wrong.

A. 🎧 When letters are used in an abbreviation, we usually stress the last letter. Listen and repeat.

| UN | WHO | ER | OR | TV | DVD | BA | BS | MA | PhD | MD |

B. 🎧 Listen and repeat each sentence.

He's in the ER. A doctor from the OR is coming to look at him.
Is he an MD or a PhD?
He's a PhD. He works for the UN.
Are you watching TV or are you watching a movie on your DVD?
She has a BS and an MA in history.

C. PAIRS Change the underlined words to abbreviations. Then take turns reading the sentences. Stress the last letter of each abbreviation.

A four-year college gives a <u>Bachelor of Arts</u> or <u>Bachelor of Science</u> degree.
It's hard to get into the <u>Master of Arts</u> program.
The ambulance will take her to the <u>emergency room</u> of the nearest hospital.
They're taking him to the <u>operating room</u>.
Her <u>medical degree</u> is from Harvard University.
The <u>World Health Organization</u> is part of the <u>United Nations</u>.

Listening Comprehension 1

Warm up: Pirates sailed oceans, attacked other boats, and stole things from them. What do pirates make you think of?

🎧 We usually think of a skull and crossbones as the flag of pirates. But there are other pirate flags. Listen to a talk about pirate flags. All these statements are false. Change them to true statements.

1. A blue flag with a skull and crossbones is called the "Jolly Roger."
2. The Jolly Roger was the flag of British and French pirates.
3. Some pirate flags showed hearts with love pouring from them.
4. Some pirate flags had clocks on them.
5. Pirates tried to show they were not angry about death.
6. Today, a skull and crossbones is a sign of good luck.

A. PAIRS Match the phrases with the definition. Write the letter of the definition next to the phrase. (The answers are on page 107.)

1. chilled to the bone _____   a. study

2. have a bone to pick _____   b. sense something

3. make no bones about it _____   c. very cold

4. feel it in my bones _____   d. be very thin

5. all skin and bones _____   e. very dry

6. dry as a bone _____   f. tell what you think without feeling ashamed about it

7. bone up on (something) _____   g. tell someone that you are annoyed and want to talk about it

B. PAIRS Complete the sentences with the correct phrase from **A**. Check your answers on page 107. Then take turns reading each sentence to your partner.

1. We haven't had rain for weeks. Everything is _____.

2. After that long walk in the cold we were _____.

3. I _____ with you. You always mispronounce my name. It's not that hard.

4. I can _____. Something is not right.

5. We _____. We charge a lot of money, but our work is good.

6. We plan to visit Mexico. I need to _____ my Spanish.

7. When he returned from the hospital, he was _____.

Listening Comprehension 2

Warm up: How many ways do we use X-rays today?

B. 🎧 **Listen to this talk about X-rays and answer the questions.**

Whose hand did Roentgen X-ray for his experiments?
When did Roentgen win the Nobel Prize in physics?
What are three uses for X-rays?
Why did Roentgen choose the name "X-ray"?

Check This Out

GROUPS Can you understand these three symbols?

Do you think these symbols show what they intend to show? Why or why not? Can you design a better symbol?

Unit 25 — Years Ago: Childhood Memories

In many parts of the world, children play games with chalk and games with rope.
Did you play such games? If so, what games did you play?

Facts

A. GROUPS Guess which statements are true (T) and which statements are false (F).

<u>Your answer</u>   <u>Were you right?</u>

_____	1. Something for children to play with is called a tie.	_____
_____	2. Something children play with that looks like a small person is called a baby.	_____
_____	3. Worldwide sales of computer and video games in 2002 were over 10 million dollars.	_____
_____	4. When children play "make-believe" games, they pretend to be someone they aren't.	_____
_____	5. When the puppet Pinocchio told a lie, his ears grew.	_____
_____	6. Most adults can't remember things that happened before the age of two and a half.	_____

🎧 **Now listen and check your answers. Change the false statements to true ones.**

B. GROUPS
- Take turns saying the facts. Then close your books.
- How many facts can you remember? Say all the facts you remember.

Talk about Your Experience

A. PAIRS Answer the questions. Then ask your partner. Add information.

Example: A: *When I played a make-believe game, I pretended to be a superhero.*
B: *Which one?*
A: *Superman. What about you?*
B: *I pretended to be a doctor.*

	YOU	YOUR PARTNER

• When I played a make-believe game, I pretended to be _____.
  • a superhero
  • a prince/princess
  • a warrior
  • a movie/TV character
  • a doctor/nurse/teacher/mother/father
• When I was a child, I used to:
  • wear _____
  • play _____
  • eat a lot of _____
  • go to _____
  • hate _____
  • collect _____
  • read _____		

B. WHOLE CLASS Choose a favorite childhood TV show, toy, game, movie, or sport. Write five sentences about it. Tell the class.

Example: *When I was a child, my favorite game was soccer. I played soccer for five hours every day. My parents always wanted me to study, but I wanted to play soccer. Then I got a soccer scholarship. My parents were happy.*

Give Your Opinion

A. Listen to these opinions.

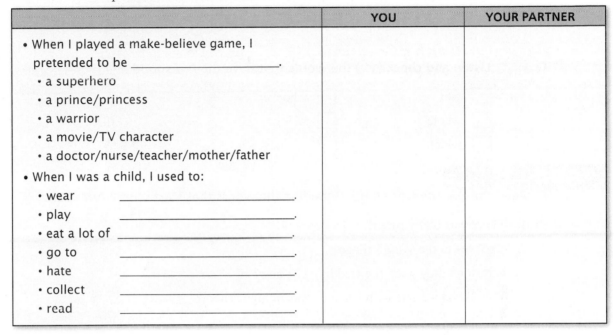

Children have too much schoolwork today.

It's more fun to be a child than an adult.

Children learn as much from playing as they do from school.

Electronic toys are the best.

B. PAIRS Take turns. Student A reads an opinion. Student B responds and adds information.

Example: A: *Children have too much schoolwork today.*
B: *I disagree. I think it's good for children to do a lot of schoolwork. It makes it easy for them to work hard later.*
A: *You must be kidding. Children need to play. They get much too much schoolwork. Most schoolwork is a waste of time.*

Responses
Strong Agreement and Disagreement
You're absolutely right.
You must be kidding.

Pronunciation Pointer — The /w/ Sound

A. Listen to these words. The "w" is pronounced.

| what | where | when | why |

B. Listen to these words. The "w" is **not** pronounced.

| who | write | wrong | wrap |

C. Listen and check (✓) the words that have the /w/ sound.

- [ ] why
- [ ] whole
- [ ] which
- [ ] wreck
- [ ] whoever
- [ ] wring
- [ ] whenever

D. Read these sentences aloud. Underline the words that start with a /w/ sound.

1. Where was that written?
2. Who was in the West Village?
3. Why don't they wrap the wedding gift now?
4. Who did he wrestle with when he was in high school?

Listening Comprehension 1

PAIRS Listen to the conversation. Circle the game the people are playing. Explain why you think so.

| soccer | tennis | basketball | baseball | volleyball | hockey |

Conversation Practice

GROUPS List some games you played as a child. Find one that your partners don't know. Answer your partners' questions about the game.

Examples: *Marco Polo, Go Fish, Steal the Bacon*

> A: *Do you know "Steal the Bacon"?*
> B: *Yes, I do.*
> A: *How about "Go Fish"?*
> B: *No, I don't know "Go Fish." What kind of game is it?*
> A: *It's a card game.*
> B: *How many people can play it?*
> A: *Up to four.*

Questions about Games:

What kind of a game is it?
How many people can play the game?
How do you keep score?

What do you need to play?
What do you need to do to win?

Warm up: The Museum of Childhood Memories is in Wales. What do you think is in a museum with that name?

🎧 **Listen and check (✓) what they have at this museum.**

- ☐ action figures
- ☐ bicycles
- ☐ rocking horses
- ☐ computer games
- ☐ doll houses
- ☐ teddy bears
- ☐ puppets

Check This Out

*"Grandma had a favorite doll when she was your age.
But, with no explanation, that doll was taken away from her and
sent to live with some cousins in Wichita."*

GROUPS What happened to the grandmother? About how many years ago did it happen? Why is she still upset? Is that funny? Why or why not?

Did anyone ever break one of your toys or take one away from you? Were you upset?
Can you remember something from your childhood that upset you? What happened? Can you laugh about it today?

Unit 26

Zippers, Buttons, and Velcro: Clothes and Fashion

Do you like this outfit?
Do you like to wear unusual clothes?

Facts

A. GROUPS Try to complete the sentences.

Were you right?

1. The first zipper was shown at the Chicago World's Fair in the _____.

   a. 1850s   b. 1870s   c. 1890s   d. 1920s   _____

2. In 1952 the first Velcro company was started in _____.

   a. Sweden   b. France   c. Switzerland   d. Germany   _____

3. Fashionable clothes are in _____.

   a. time   b. sync   c. style   d. a row   _____

4. All of the following are fabrics except _____.

   a. cotton   b. wool   c. nylon   d. jeans   _____

5. All of the following are clothes only for women except a _____.

   a. dress   b. skirt   c. vest   d. blouse   _____

6. A _____ alters clothes.

   a. tailor   b. sailor   c. whaler   d. jailor   _____

🎧 **Now listen and check your answers.**

B. GROUPS
* Take turns saying the facts. Then close your books.
* How many facts can you remember? Say all the facts you remember.

Talk about Your Experience

A. PAIRS Answer the questions. Then ask your partner. Add information.

Example: A: *Can you sew?*
              B: *Yes, I can. I learned to sew in the army. What about you?*
              A: *I can't sew.*

	YOU	YOUR PARTNER

• Can you sew? If so, what can you sew?
When a button falls off, what do you do?
 	
• Where do you like to shop for clothes?
Department stores? Chain stores? Flea markets?
Boutiques?
Why? What brands do you like? Why?
 	
• What is most important when you buy clothes?
  • Style?
  • Comfort?
  • Price?		

B. WHOLE CLASS What is in style this season for women? For men? Do you like the new styles? Why or why not?

Give Your Opinion

A. 🎧 Listen to these opinions.

Most people dress for others.

People judge you by your clothes.

T-shirts, jeans, and running shoes are the best clothes.

Clothes are not important.

B. GROUPS Take turns. Read an opinion. Each student responds and adds information.

Example: A: *Most people dress for others.*
              B: *I suppose. Most people wear whatever is popular. This year*
                 almost everyone is wearing gray. That's because it's an
                 "in" color. I think people are afraid to look too different.
              C: *I'm not sure about that. There are some people who have*
                 their own style. They only wear what looks good on them.

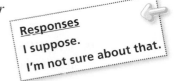

Responses
I suppose.
I'm not sure about that.

A. 🎧 Listen to these sentences. Notice the stress. Then listen again and repeat.

It's too **big**.	They're too **big**.
It's too **tight**.	They're too **tight**.
It doesn't **work**.	They don't **work**.
It doesn't **match**.	They don't **match**.
It's too **small**.	They're too **small**.
It's too **loose**.	They're too **loose**.
It doesn't **fit**.	They don't **fit**.
It doesn't **close**.	They don't **close**.

B. PAIRS Take turns. Point to a picture. Ask what's wrong with the clothes. Your partner responds with a sentence from above.

Example: A: *What's wrong with the shoes?*
                 B: *They're too big.*

Listening Comprehension 1

A. 🎧 Listen to a conversation between two friends. Then listen again, and complete the compliments (things they say to show they admire each other).

1. That sweater _____.

2. I love _____.

3. I like _____.

4. You're _____.

B. WHOLE CLASS Walk around the classroom, and compliment your classmates.

Conversation Practice

A. GROUPS How many things use Velcro? How many things use zippers? Add to the lists.

Velcro	Zippers
wallets	*wallets*
shoes	*suitcases*

B. GROUPS Talk about advantages and disadvantages of zippers and velcro.

Example: *I think velcro is good for clothes for the very young and the very old. Velcro is easier for them to use than buttons or laces.*

Warm up: What's your favorite clothing invention?

Galoshes

🎧 **Listen and fill in the blanks.**

The Story of the Zipper

Whitcomb Judson got a patent for the zipper in _____. But this zipper didn't _____ and nobody _____ it. Judson showed it to _____ of people at the Chicago World's Fair. He sold only _____ zippers.

In 1913, Gideon Sundback made a _____ zipper. But this zipper did not _____ well either. Then _____ years later, B.F. Goodrich became interested in the zipper. That's when zippers _____ to sell.

At that time, B.F. Goodrich had a new product for the _____. He made rubber boots to protect people from the _____. He called these boots "galoshes." He liked the _____ and _____ 150,000 for his galoshes. After that zippers sold everywhere.

C. WHOLE CLASS Have you ever worn galoshes?

Check This Out

GROUPS Men and women of all ages spend a lot of time and money fixing their hair. Why? How much time do you spend each day fixing your hair? How often do you go to a beauty salon or barber?

"I love it. Who did it?"

Unit 1

Student A: You and your partner want to fly from Tokyo to Honolulu. Ask your partner questions about the United Airlines flight. Answer your partner's questions about the Northwest Airlines flight.

> *Example:* A: When does the United Airlines flight leave Tokyo?
> B: It leaves from Narita Airport at 7:30 PM.

UNITED AIRLINES

Departs	Arrives	Travel Time	Price
Time: Tokyo, Japan Narita (NRT)	Time: Honolulu, HI (HNL)	___ hrs. ___ min.	Roundtrip: $ _____

NORTHWEST AIRLINES

Departs	Arrives	Travel Time	Price
8:40 pm Tokyo, Japan Narita (NRT)	8:55 am Honolulu, HI (HNL)	7 hrs. 15 min.	Roundtrip: $ 1104

B. Now work together, and answer these questions.

1. Which trip is longer? later? more expensive?

Unit 7

PAIRS Ask your partner questions to complete the Summer Olympic Games chart. Answer your partner's questions about the Winter Olympic Games.

> *Examples:* A: When were the 14th Summer Olympic Games held?
> B: In 1948.

Summer Olympic Games

14th	_____	London, England
15th	1952	_____
16th	1956	_____
17th	_____	Rome, Italy
18th	1964	_____
19th	_____	Mexico City, Mexico

Winter Olympic Games

	Year	Place
14th	1984	Sarajevo, Yugoslavia
15th	1988	Calgary, Canada
16th	1992	Albertville, France
17th	1994	Lillehammer, Norway
18th	1998	Nagano, Japan
19th	2002	Salt Lake City, U. S. A

Unit 18

Ask your partner about the temperature and weather in these South American and Asian/Pacific cities. Answer your partner's questions.

> *Example:* A: What's the weather like in Buenos Aires?
> B: It's sunny.
> A: What's the temperature in Buenos Aires?
> B: It's 15 degrees.

$(F° - 32) \times 5/9 = C°$

$(9/5 \times C°) + 32 = F°$

Today's Weather	
South America Buenos Aires – Lima – Rio de Janeiro –	**Asia/Pacific** Bangkok – Hong Kong – Sydney –
North America Acapulco – 33° partly cloudy New York – 25° partly cloudy Vancouver – 20° rainy	**Europe** Budapest – 27° sunny Geneva – 34° sunny Moscow – 28° sunny

Answers to Selected Exercises

Unit 4

Check This Out

The sum of the four numbers is 52.
Call the first number n.
The next number is n+1.
The next number is n +7 and the next number is n +8.

Add up the four numbers:
n+n+1+n+7+n+8

Those numbers equal 52.

n+n+1+n+7+n+8=52
4n+16=52
4n=36
n=9   (1st day)
n+1=10   (2nd day)
n+7=16   (3rd day)
n+8=17   (4th day)

Unit 6

Listening Comprehension 1

In-line skating

Unit 8

Conversation Practice

1. A "get well soon" card.

2. A dance.

3. A "swcct sixtccn" party.

4. A "housewarming gift."

Unit 19

Check This Out

1. b

2. a

3. c

Unit 24

Knee

Conversation Practice

A.

1. c   5. d

2. g   6. e

3. f   7. a

4. b

B.

1. dry as a bone

2. chilled to the bone

3. have a bone to pick

4. feel it in my bones

5. made no bones about it

6. bone up on

7. all skin and bones

Information Gap Student B

Unit 1

Student B: You and your partner want to fly from Tokyo to Honolulu. Answer your partner's questions about the United Airlines flight. Ask your partner questions about the Northwest Airlines flight.

Example: B: *When does the Northwest Airlines flight leave Tokyo?*
A: *It leaves from Narita Airport at 8:40 PM.*

UNITED AIRLINES

Departs	Arrives	Travel Time	Price
7:30 pm Tokyo, Japan Narita (NRT)	7:45 am Honolulu, HI (HNL)	7 hrs. 15 min.	Roundtrip: $ 978

NORTHWEST AIRLINES

Departs	Arrives	Travel Time	Price
Time: Tokyo, Japan Narita (NRT)	Time: Honolulu, HI (HNL)	__ hrs. __ min.	Roundtrip: $ _____

B. Now work together, and answer these questions.

Which trip is longer? later? more expensive?

Unit 7

PAIRS Answer your partner's questions about the Summer Olympic Games. Then ask your partner questions to complete the Winter Olympic Games held?

Examples: A: *Where were the 14th Winter Olympic Games held?*
B: *In Sarajevo, Yugoslavia.*

Winter Olympic Games

	Year	Place
14th	1948	London, England
15th	1952	Helsinki, Finland
16th	1956	Melbourne, Australia
17th	1960	Rome, Italy
18th	1964	Tokyo, Japan
19th	1968	Mexico City, Mexico

Winter Olympic Games

14th	1984	_____
15th	_____	Calgary, Canada
16th	1992	_____
17th	1994	_____
18th	_____	Nagano, Japan
19th	2002	_____

Unit 18

Answer your partner's questions. Ask your partner about the temperature and weather in these North American and European cities.

Example: A: *What's the weather like in Acapulco?*
B: *It's partly cloudy.*
A: *What's the temperature in Acapulco?*
B: *It's 33 degrees.*

$$(F° - 32) \times 5/9 = C°$$
$$(9/5 \times C°) + 32 = F°$$

Today's Weather	
South America Buenos Aires – 15° sunny Lima – 18° partly cloudy Rio de Janeiro – 24° sunny	**Asia/Pacific** Bangkok – 31° partly cloudy Hong Kong – 35° partly cloudy Sydney – 18° sunny
North America Acapulco – New York – Vancouver –	**Europe** Budapest – Geneva – Moscow –

Tapescript

Unit 1 Air Travel

Page 2 Facts

A

1. A plane takes off and lands.
2. You can travel first class, business class, or coach.
3. After traveling a long distance in a plane, many people have jet lag.
4. The world's busiest airport is Chicago O'Hare.
5. The first flight attendants were single, female nurses.
6. In 1987 American Airlines saved $40,000. The airline stopped putting an olive in each salad in first class.

Page 4 Listening Comprehension 1

Attention please. Due to weather conditions, the following flights from Vancouver have been canceled.
Japan Airlines Flight 15 to Tokyo Narita, and United Airlines flight #8624 to New York JFK. Also due to weather conditions, the following flights from Vancouver have been delayed. Air Canada flight 776 to Honolulu and Aeromexico flight 9312 to Acapulco. For more information, please go to the check-in counter of your airline. Thank you, and we are sorry for any inconvenience.

Page 5 Listening Comprehension 2

A: Can I help you?
B: Yes, thank you. I'd like a round trip ticket from New York to Miami for next Sunday.
A: Is that the 21st of February?
B: Yes, it is.
A: That'll be $400.
B: $400? You advertise a round trip ticket for $110.
A: Oh. That's only on weekdays.
B: Well then I'll fly on Monday the 22nd of February.
A: I'm sorry. To get that price, you need to reserve your ticket a month in advance.
B: Hmm. Well then, I'll take a round trip ticket for March 22. How's that?
A: Okay. Let me check the computer. I'm so sorry. We're sold out for that day. How about April 22?
B: April 22? I wanted to get away from the cold weather in New York in February. It's not cold in April! I don't want to leave New York in April. Sorry.

Unit 2 Breakfast

Page 6 Facts

A

1. "Brunch" is a combination of breakfast and lunch.
2. Many people in the US and Canada eat "fast food" for breakfast.
3. "Expresso" is strong coffee.
4. When you "fast," you don't eat anything. The word breakfast" comes from "breaking (ending) the fast" of the night.
5. In many Asian countries, rice is a part of breakfast.
6. In Japan, people often have rice and miso soup as part of breakfast.

Page 8 Listening Comprehension 1

Server: Are you ready to order?
Man: I think we are. I'd like the pancakes and coffee.
Server: Okay. And you?
Woman: I'd like eggs with toast and jelly.
Server: How do you want the eggs?
Woman: Scrambled.
Server: Would you like something to drink?
Woman: I'd like apple juice and tea. Do you have green tea?
Server: Yes, we do.
Woman: Great.
Server: Will that be all?
Man: Yes. Thank you.

Page 9 Listening Comprehension 2

Online Survey: Breakfast in Japan

An online survey about breakfast went to 5000 people. Three hundred and sixty seven people answered the questions, all of them Japanese people living in Japan. About three-quarters of those who answered were women under 30 years old.
The first question was, "What style breakfast do you usually have?" Twenty percent said Japanese, and twenty-four percent said Western. Forty percent said that they eat a mixed Western and Japanese breakfast, and thirteen percent said they don't eat breakfast.
Next, they were asked, "How much time do you spend eating breakfast? Six percent said they spend from 2 to 5 minutes. Twenty-four percent spend from five to ten minutes. The largest number, thirty five percent said they spend between 10 and 15 minutes eating breakfast. Eighteen percent spend 15 to 20 minutes, and only six percent said they spend over 20 minutes eating breakfast.
Another question asked about drinks with breakfast. The largest percent drink different kinds of tea. Thirty five percent said they drink milk. Thirty-two percent said coffee, thirty-one percent said green tea, twenty-one percent said English tea, and eleven percent said they drink orange juice.
The final question asked what they do while eating breakfast. The largest number, seventy two percent, said they watch television. Twenty-seven percent said they read a newspaper. Twenty-three percent said they talk, twelve percent listen to news on the radio, and only six percent listen to music.

Unit 3 Colors

Page 10 Facts

A

1. Brides wear red in traditional Chinese weddings.
2. The three primary colors are red, blue, and yellow.
3. A jealous person is green with envy.
4. When you're sad, you feel blue.
5. White is a combination of all colors.
6. If you combine red and blue, you get purple.

Page 12 Listening Comprehension 1

John: So Helena, how will I recognize you?
Helena: I have blond hair and green eyes.
John: Blond hair and blue eyes.
Helena: Green eyes.
John: Oh, like grass.
Helena: I guess. And I'll be wearing a red jacket. What about you, John? How will I know who you are?
John: Well, my hair is dark brown and my eyes are brown too. I'm wearing a white sweatshirt.
Helena: Was that a white sweater?
John: No, a white sweatshirt.
Helena: Okay.
John: Great. So, you're on flight 37, which arrives at 10:10, right?
Helena: That's right. We can meet at the baggage claim area.
John: All right. See you then. And if there's a problem, you have my cell phone number, right?
Helena: Right. See you.

Page 13 Listening Comprehension 2

A

"M & M's" is an American candy. The inside is chocolate and the outside is a sugar coating that comes in different colors. A few years ago, the makers of "M & M's" added a new color. Blue. Blue? Why blue? It was a result of a vote by M & M's fans. But it is likely that the blue candy will be the last one left in the bag.

Of all the different colors, blue is the least appetizing. Dieters are told to put food on a blue plate or to put a blue light in their refrigerator.

Why does blue take away the appetite? It's because blue food is rare in nature. There are no blue vegetables, no blue meats, and aside from blueberries, blue almost never is a natural food color. Also, years ago when people searched for food, they learned that blue, purple, and black were often a sign of bad food.

The color and a food's appeal are closely related. Some foods fail in the marketplace because of their color, not their taste.

Unit 4 Days, Months, and Numbers

Page 14 Facts

A

1. A decade is ten years.
2. A century is one hundred years.
3. In Japan, Korea, and China, the number four is considered unlucky.
4. When a baby is born in Korea, it is one year old.
5. People in most countries read the date 3/6 as June 3. In other countries they read it as March 6.
6. Chinese New Year is sometimes in January and sometimes in February. It is based on a lunar calendar.

Page 16 Listening Comprehension 1

A: What's your phone number?
B: It's 917-555-9072.
A: Sorry. Could you say it more slowly? I'd like to write it down.
B: Sure. It's 9-1-7.
A: Got it.
B: 5-5-5.
A: OK.
B: 9-0-7-2.

A: 9070?
B: No. 9072.
A: Oh. Let me just repeat it. 917-555-9072.
B: That's right.
A: Thank you. And what's your address?
B: It's 14 Jane Street.
A: Is that fourteen or forty?
B: Fourteen.
A: So it's 14 Jane Street.
B: That's right. "J" as in "jet."
A: Thank you.

Page 17 Listening Comprehension 2

Coincidences

A: I met a guy last weekend. It turns out we were born on the same day, the same month, and the same year.
B: What a coincidence!

When two things happen together by chance, in a surprising way, we call it a coincidence.

In 1992 there was a contest. It asked people to find coincidences between presidents. Arturo Magidín of Mexico City won the contest. He came up with 16 coincidences between former U.S. President Kennedy and former Mexican President Alvaro Obregón. Here are some of the coincidences:

The names "Kennedy" and "Obregón" have seven letters each.
    Both men were assassinated.
    Both their assassins had three names.
    Both their assassins died soon after killing the president.
    Both Kennedy and Obregón were married in years ending in 3.
    Both Kennedy and Obregón had a son who died soon after birth.
    Both men came from large families.
    Both men died in their forties.
Do the similarities between Kennedy and Obregón surprise you?

Unit 5 E-mail and the Internet

Page 18 Facts

A

1. Today we talk about two types of mail, e-mail and snail mail.
2. A laptop is a computer you can carry with you.
3. The letters BTW in an e-mail message mean *by the way*.
4. The "e" in e-mail stands for electronic.
5. Your personal e-mail location is called your e-mail address.
6. When you are connected to the Internet, you are online.

Page 20 Listening Comprehension 1

Amy: Sam, why do we use the word "bug" for a computer problem?
Sam: There is a story I heard: In 1945 a computer at Harvard University didn't work. Grace Hopper was working on the computer. She decided to look into the problem. She found a moth in the computer. She removed the moth and the computer worked without a problem. Since then when something goes wrong with a computer, we say, "There's a bug in the computer."
Ellen: That sounds good Sam, but that's not exactly true. They used the word "bug" for problems a long time before that.
Sam: Oh well, it's a good story.

Reporter:	Good afternoon. We are asking people for their opinion of the Internet. Do you mind answering a few questions?
Man:	Not at all.
Reporter:	Thank you. Do you use the Internet? And do you like it?
Man:	Yes, to both questions. I use the Internet. And I think it's great. I'm a medical doctor. I can learn about the latest ideas in medicine. I also use e-mail all the time.
Reporter:	Is there anything you don't like about the Internet?
Man:	Well sometimes the Internet causes problems between my patients and me. Some patients read articles on the Internet and think they know all about their diseases. And they tell me what medicine they need.
Reporter:	Really?
Man:	Uh-huh. Just last week, a man came to see me. He said, "I checked the Internet and I'm sure I have cancer." He didn't.
Reporter:	Well, I can see that that's a problem. Thank you so much for this interview.
Man:	You're welcome.

Unit 6 *Fears and Phobias*

Page 22 Facts

A

1. To fear something is to be afraid of it.
2. When you're very scared, you might say, "I'm scared to death."
3. An actor is nervous before a play. He has stage fright.
4. Someone is nervous before an event. She says, "I have butterflies in my stomach."
5. Phobias are strong fears of things that are not really dangerous. Phobias such as a fear of flying are most common in women.
6. Social phobias, such as a fear of meeting new people, are equally common in men and women.

Page 24 Listening Comprehension 1

A: I can't do it.
B: Sure you can.
A: No. I'm afraid.
B: Don't worry. You have a helmet, and knee and elbow pads. You won't get hurt. Just take one step at a time. Like this. Watch me. It's fun.
A: Like this?
B: That's it. Now move the other foot. Bend your knees.
A: How's this?
B: Great.
A: Hey! It's fun.
B: I told you so.

Page 25 Listening Comprehension 2

Dear Sad & Lonely,

It's really hard to move to a new town during high school. And it's especially difficult for someone who is quiet and afraid to meet people. But here are a few hints. I hope they work.

Find one classmate you are comfortable with. Call and ask that person about a class, homework, or a test.

Invite someone to your home.

Join a club that has an activity you like, or form a club if there isn't one.

Use the Internet to get to know classmates. E-mail them and chat on line. It may be easier for you than face-to-face meetings.

Be patient. It takes time to make friends.

I really hope these hints help. And please let me know what happens.

Sincerely yours,
Frieda

Unit 7 *Games and Sports*

Page 26 Facts

A

1. Golf began in Scotland.
2. A "good sport," doesn't get angry about losing.
3. The Olympics began in Greece.
4. A marathon is a race of about 26 miles.
5. "Love" means no points in tennis.
6. A king, a queen, and a knight are part of a chess game.

Page 28 Listening Comprehension 1

1. The first modern Olympic Games took place in Athens, Greece in 1896. There were 70,000 people in the stadium.
2. Olympic Games take place every four years, but in 1916 and in 1944, the Games were canceled due to war.
3. The first Winter Olympics were in 1924 in Chamonix, France. In 1980 the 13th Winter Olympic Games took place in Lake Placid in the United States.

Page 29 Listening Comprehension 2

A: Is he really called "Tiger"?
B: Yes. However, for the record, his real name is Eldrick Woods.
A: How tall is Tiger? And how much does he weigh?
B: He's 6'2". He weighs 156 pounds.
A: When was he born?
B: December 30, 1975. He has no brothers or sisters.
A: What is Tiger's background?
B: His father is half black, one-quarter American Indian and one quarter Chinese. His mother is half Thai, one-quarter Chinese and one-quarter white. His father was an officer in the Army.
A: Where's Tiger's hometown?
B: He grew up in Cypress, California, south-east of Los Angeles.
A: What kind of schooling did he have?
B: He was a student at Stanford University, but left in his third year to become a professional golfer.
A: How did he get started playing?
B: Like most kids, he got introduced to the game by his dad, Earl Woods. However, his dad makes it clear that he raised Tiger to be a golfing star.
A: Why does Tiger wear the color red on the final day of a tournament?
B: Tiger wears red because his mother feels that it is a "power color" for Tiger.

Unit 8 *Holidays and Special Occasions*

Page 30 Facts

A

1. Labor Day is a holiday for workers.
2. People celebrate their anniversary on the day they were married.
3. Ch'suk is an important holiday in Korea. It's like the American Thanksgiving.

4. New Year's Eve is the night before New Year's Day.
5. Teacher's Day is not a holiday in the United States.
6. People get a bachelor's degree when they graduate from a four-year college.
7. In Brazil during Carnaval, people wear costumes and sing in the streets.

Page 32 Listening Comprehension 1

Maria: John, I need your help. I've got to get a gift for my Dad. It's his 60th birthday, and I can't decide on a gift. What do you think? Should I get him a camera or a DVD player?
John: Well, what does he like more, watching movies or taking pictures?
Maria: I guess taking pictures.
John: So get him the camera.
Maria: Okay. Now what do you think, digital or regular?
John: Digital. They're a lot of fun.
Maria: One more question. Do you think I should ask him first or surprise him?
John: Surprise him. He can always return it.
Maria: Thanks. You've been a real help.

Page 32 Conversation Practice

1. You send a sick friend a "get well soon" card.
2. A "prom" is a dance that takes place at the end of students' last year of high school.
3. A sixteen-year-old girl has a "sweet sixteen" party.
4. A gift for a new home is called a "housewarming" gift.

Page 33 Listening Comprehension 2

Dr. Julian Ford is a psychologist at the University of Connecticut. He says that many people feel stress and often have too much to do around the holidays. He offers advice to make holidays easier. Here are a few of his suggestions:

Decide what's most important for you.
If your gift list is too long, give a gift certificate.
Shop on the Internet or from catalogues.
Don't do it all yourself. Do some jobs with someone else, not just by yourself.
Don't eat, drink, or party too much.
Gift giving is not about money. Try to stay within your budget. Don't spend more than you have.

Unit 9 Ice Cream and Other Desserts

Page 34 Facts

A

1. People usually end a meal with dessert.
2. Flan is a popular dessert in Spain and Mexico
3. Tiramisu is a popular dessert from Italy.
4. 80% of the world's Vanilla bean is grown in Madagascar.
5. The most popular ice cream flavor in the United States is vanilla.
6. In Brazil desserts are often made with guava, avocado, mango, and coconut.

Page 36 Listening Comprehension 1

A: Mmm, Jan. This cake is really good
B: Thanks. It was easy to make.
A: Oh yeah? It's so light. What's in it?
B: Well, there's flour of course. And sugar, cocoa, baking soda.

A: Any eggs?
B: No, there aren't any eggs. There's a little salt, water, and vegetable oil.
A: Is that it?
B: I think so. No... I forgot. There's vinegar and vanilla. That's all. If you want the recipe, I'll write it down.
A: Thanks.

Page 37 Listening Comprehension 2

1. Ice cream was invented in China around 4,000 years ago when the Chinese packed a soft milk and rice mixture in snow.
2. The Roman Emperor Nero sent slaves to the mountains to bring fresh snow to his kitchens. The snow was flavored with fruits and honey.
3. In 1812 in the United States, Dolly Madison, the President's wife, served ice cream at an important ball. It was a big hit.
4. The ice cream cone was first introduced at the St. Louis World's Fair in 1904.
5. The top five consumers of ice cream are: the United States, New Zealand, Denmark, Australia, and Belgium.

Unit 10 Jazz and Other Types of Music

Page 38 Facts

A

1. Jazz started among slaves from West Africa.
2. A popular type of music in which the words are spoken, not sung, is called rap.
3. The leader of an orchestra is called a conductor.
4. When we hear something we like, we say, "That's music to my ears."
5. The music of Bach, Beethoven, and Mozart is called classical music.
6. Traditional music played by the ordinary people of an area is called folk music.

Page 40 Listening Comprehension 1

1. This is a famous symphony by Beethoven. Some say it is the sound of your future knocking on the door. It's Beethoven's Fifth Symphony.
2. This song was sung by the Beatles. The title is a past time word. The song is called "Yesterday."
3. Many young people in the United States sang this song in the 1960s. The name of the song is "We Shall Overcome."
4. At Princess Diana's funeral, Elton John sang, " Candle in the Wind."
5. This popular movie starring Sylvester Stallone is about a boxer. The name of the boxer and the movie is *Rocky*.

Page 41 Listening Comprehension 2

Like Jazz, Brazilian music has African roots. Samba is the most popular Brazilian rhythm. It is related to music that African slaves brought to Brazil.
In the early 1960s, Joao Gilberto and Antonio Carlos Jobim developed the Bossa Nova, a slower kind of Samba. Then they began to mix jazz and Bossa Nova. Two American musicians visited Brazil in the 1960s. They were Stan Getz and Charlie Byrd. They fell in love with the music of Jobim and Gilberto and brought it to North America. Soon people all over the world began to play their music.
In 1963 Getz and Gilberto made a record that was sold all over the world. But the most popular song on their record was by Gilberto's wife, Astrud, who sang "The Girl from Ipanema." That song became known to millions and is still heard throughout the world.

Unit 11 Kangaroos, Koalas, and Australia

Page 42 Facts

A

1. The capital of Australia is Canberra.
2. The Great Barrier Reef is the largest coral structure in the world.
3. Koalas are related to kangaroos.
4. Baby kangaroos and baby koala bears travel in their mother's pouch.
5. Koalas eat mostly the leaves of the eucalyptus tree.
6. Baby kangaroos are called joeys.
7. Paul Hogan starred in the Australian movie called *Crocodile Dundee*.

Page 44 Listening Comprehension 1

A: This is the famous Sydney Opera House.
B: It's amazing. Is there a place to eat here?
A: Yes. You can eat here. And you can do other things here too.
B: Like what?
A: You can see dance performances and plays. And you can hear concerts of jazz and pop music.
B: Do they show movies too?
A: No, you can't see movies, but you can listen to talks.
B: It's big enough for sports events. Are there any sports events?
A: No, you can't watch sports events or play sports here.
B: Still, it's awesome.

Page 44 Conversation Practice

A

1. A kangaroo can't hop 60 kilometers per hour (40 miles per hour).
2. A kangaroo can weigh up to 85 kilograms.
3. A kangaroo can't walk or move backwards.
4. A kangaroo can live with very little water.
5. Most kangaroos can't move their legs one at a time.

Page 45 Listening Comprehension 2

Uluru is one of the biggest rocks in the world. The rock is very important to native Australians for religious reasons. It is located in a National Park in the Northern Territory of Australia. It used to be called Ayers Rock. You can climb it or walk around it. The climb up the rock is 345 meters and the walk around it is 9.4 kilometers. The rock is in the shape of an oval. It changes color in the light and is most beautiful at sunrise and sunset.

William Gosse was the first to write about the rock in 1873. He named it Ayers rock for Sir Henry Ayers. Sir Henry Ayers was the South Australian premier at that time. In 1995 the name of the National Park was changed to show the native Australian ownership and relationship to the area.

Unit 12 Love

Page 46 Facts

A

1. On Valentine's Day in Japan, women give men chocolates.
2. A romantic idea is often not practical.
3. A matchmaker introduces people for the purpose of arranging marriages.
4. When a man asks a woman to marry him, he often says, "Will you marry me?"
5. A blind date is a date with a person you have never met before.
6. People fall in love.
7. A person who disappoints you in love "breaks your heart."

Page 48 Listening Comprehension 1

Lilly: Hi, Rita? It's me Lilly.
Rita: Hi, Lilly. What's up?
Lilly: I had dinner with my cousin Ron and I want you to meet him.
Rita: Oh yeah?
Lilly: I think you will really like him.
Rita: Well, what's he like?
Lilly: He's very funny. He has a great sense of humor. He works for an advertising agency. And on weekends he likes to go hiking.
Rita: That sounds good. What does he look like?
Lilly: He's very tall and nicely built. He has light brown hair and a cute mustache. I have a picture of him and his friends. Do you want me to e-mail it to you?
Rita: Sure.

Page 49 Listening Comprehension 2

Dear Clara,

Mike and I fell in love last summer. We have a great time together, and we agree on most things. He's a doctor. I'm a writer, and a part-time assistant in Mike's office. We're planning to marry in June. Our families get along well, and we've never had a fight until last week. Last week he told me he wants me to sign a legal paper. It says that if our marriage ends in the next ten years, I will not get any money from him.

Now I'm very upset. I think it's awful that he wants me to sign such a paper. I still love him, but I don't know what to do. I never would ask him to sign such a letter, and it's not because I have no money. I wrote a novel six years ago which was quite successful. I have a lot of money.

What do you think?

Jennifer

Unit 13 Movies

Page 50 Facts

A

1. The person with the main role in a movie is the "star" of the movie.
2. *Titanic* was a popular movie about a shipwreck.
3. When a film's words are spoken in another language, we say the movie is dubbed.
4. Steven Spielberg and Akira Kurosawa are directors.
5. India makes more films than any other country.
6. Very popular movies are called "blockbusters."

Page 52 Listening Comprehension 1

A: What's playing at the Cineplex this evening?
B: Well, there are four films. There's *Ma*.
A: Is that a comedy?
B: Yes, it is. It's with Jon Dandy. Mary saw it. She said it's good. Then there's *War Games*. It's an action film
A: Skip that one.
B: Okay. There's *Always Together*. It's a drama, a real tear-jerker.
A: That's a possibility. I love to cry.
B: Come on. You're not serious.
A: I am.
B: The last film is *Star Trek 10*.
A: Science fiction. It could be good.

Page 53 Listening Comprehension 2

Good evening and welcome to AZ Radio Entertainment. I'm Joe Morales with tonight's suggestions for international videos. Here are two videos you will enjoy again and again. The first is *Central Station*. It's a Brazilian-French film, made in 1998. *Central Station* tells the story of a woman and a poor boy who meet at the central train station in Rio de Janeiro. The boy's mother died, and the two try to find the boy's father. Together they travel to a distant part of Brazil. There are wonderful performances by Fernanda Montenegro, as the woman, and Vinicius de Oliveira, as the little boy. The director is Walter Salles.

The second movie is from Japan. It's called, *Shall We Dance?* It was made in 1996. This movie has something for everyone. It's funny. It's sad. It's one of a kind. It's a film about a middle-aged businessman. He dreams of a different life and finds it through ballroom dancing. The movie stars Koji Yakusho and Tamiyo Kusakari. You'll see great acting and a fine production. The director is Masayuki Suo.

Unit 14 Newspapers

Page 54 Facts

A

1. The headline (the title of a newspaper story) gives the most important news.
2. A journalist writes reports for newspapers, magazines, or television.
3. Newspapers depend on advertising.
4. Editorials give opinions, not facts.
5. Local news tells the news of the city or town of the newspaper.
6. There are fewer ads in newspapers because of the Internet.

Page 56 Listening Comprehension 1

A: Is the word *news* the plural of the word *new*?
B: I read on the Internet that news comes from the first letters of *north*, *east*, *west*, and *south*.
C: I don't think so. You can't believe everything you read. According to my dictionary, *news* comes from a French word meaning "new things."

Page 57 Listening Comprehension 2

Good morning. This is Connie Walker with news for today, Tuesday May 2. It's a sunny day, but a little cold at 45 degrees. In international news, the United Nations has declared this year to be "The Year of the Teen."
In national news the President is speaking to graduates of State College this afternoon.
Finally, in local news, there will be a street fair this Sunday from 2 to 6 PM. Main Street will be closed to cars.

Unit 15 Oceans and Beaches

Page 58 Facts

A

1. Oceans cover about 70 percent of the Earth's surface.
2. There are four oceans on Earth.
3. The Pacific Ocean is the largest ocean.
4. Seas are smaller than oceans. The largest sea is the South China Sea.
5. "Jaws" is a movie about a shark.
6. *Moby Dick* is a book about a whale.
7. At the beach people use sunscreen to prevent sunburn.

Page 60 Listening Comprehension 1

Bob: Hello.
Ali: Bob? Did I wake you?
Bob: That's okay Ali. I woke up early and fell asleep again.
Ali: Listen, Bob, would you like to go to the beach this afternoon?
Bob: It's too cold to swim in the ocean.
Ali: I know. My uncle bought a fishing boat. Would you like to go fishing?
Bob: Sounds like fun. I'd love to go.
Ali: Great. Meet me in an hour at the big dock.

Page 61 Listening Comprehension 2

Relax. Listen to the sound of the ocean.
Now raise your arms.
Move them slowly up and down.
Good. Now put your arms to your sides.
Put your feet apart.
Bend over and touch your knees.
That's good. Now come up and move your head first to the left and then to the right.
That's it. Relax.

Unit 16 Parties

Page 62 Facts

A

1. Sometimes, before a man marries, his friends have a bachelor party for him.
2. A party for a woman before she gets married is a bridal shower.
3. Everyone brings something to eat at a potluck party.
4. A party each year celebrating the day a couple got married is an anniversary party.
5. A party for a new home is a housewarming party.
6. "RSVP" on an invitation means, "Please let me know if you can come."

Page 64 Listening Comprehension 1

Hi, this is Michelle. Sorry I can't take your call. Please leave your name, number and a short message.

Message Number 1
Hi, Michelle. It's Liz. I'm having a birthday party next Saturday, May 5th. It's at Hunan Gardens at 7:30. Let me know if you can come. My number is 897-555-7658.

Message Number 2
Michelle, this is John Brown. We met at Ruby's Dance Club last month. I'm in town this weekend, and I was wondering if you'd like to go to a party with me on Saturday the 5th. My number is 918-555-9090.

Message Number 3
Hi, Michelle. This is Mom. Aunt Bea is having an anniversary party on Saturday. I really hope you can make it. Call me at your cousin Emma's house. I'll be there tonight. Her number is 918 555-2134.

Page 65 Listening Comprehension 2

A

Man: Nice party.
Woman: Yes, it is.
Man: Uh...You look familiar. Don't I know you from somewhere?
Woman: Maybe.

B

Woman: Uh... Do you work near here?
Man: Yes, I do. I work at Central Bank. What about you?
Woman: I teach kindergarten at the school across the street.
Man: Maybe that's it. Uh... Would you like something to drink?
Woman: Sure. I'd love a soda with ice.
Man: Be right back. [fade out]

Unit 17 Quizzes, Test, and Intelligence

Page 66 Facts

A

1. An IQ test measures intelligence.
2. When you copy your classmate's answers, you are cheating.
3. When you cram for a test, you do all your studying just before the test.
4. A short test is called a quiz.
5. To succeed in a test is to "pass" a test.
6. A multiple choice test lets you choose from several possible answers.

Page 68 Listening Comprehension 1

GB: Good evening. This is George Barnes. Welcome to "Prizes," everyone's favorite quiz show. Our first guest is Jan Brown. Jan, tell us about yourself.
Jan: Well, George. I'm from Austin Texas. I'm a teacher. I teach Spanish and yoga.
GB: That's a nice combination. Are you ready to begin?
Jan: Yes, I am.
GB: OK now Jan. Listen to the questions. You have five seconds to answer. You get a prize for each correct answer. Our first question is a geography question. Okay?
Jan: Yes, George.
GB: What is the capital of Kenya?
Jan: Nairobi.
GB: Right you are. You win fifty dollars. Do you want to go on?
Jan: Yes, I do.
GB: OK. What country had the first ski-through McDonald's?
Jan: Was it Sweden?
GB: Right again. This time you win dinner for two at Nino's Italian restaurant.
Jan: That's great.
GB: Do you want to continue?
Jan: Yes, I do.
GB: In what year was table tennis first played in the Olympic Games?
Jan: In 1988.
GB: You're right again. Let's see what you win—a brand new TV and DVD player! Are you ready to continue?
Jan: Yes, I am.
GB: The Aswan Dam is in what country?
Jan: Hmm. I'm sorry. I don't know.
GB: I'm sorry, too. It's in Egypt. But, you did very well. You go home with three great prizes.
Jan: Thank you very much.

Page 69 Listening Comprehension 2

Howard Gardner is a professor at Harvard University. He has written many books. In 1983 Howard Gardner wrote a book that describes different kinds of intelligence. Gardner calls them "multiple intelligences."
Before Gardner, intelligence was usually measured in two ways—

language and mathematical ability. Gardner has added other kinds. They include musical intelligence, the ability to understand and create music, and spatial intelligence, which is the ability to see in pictures. Architects and graphic artists have a lot of this type of intelligence. Gardner also includes interpersonal intelligence, which is the ability to understand other people.
Today many elementary school teachers try to use his ideas in their lessons. These teachers use activities for different ways of thinking.

Unit 18 Rain

Page 70 Facts

A

1. People use an umbrella to protect themselves from the rain.
2. The humidity is high before it rains.
3. A light rain is called a "drizzle."
4. After it rains, you can sometimes see a rainbow in the sky.
5. Rain can form puddles.
6. Mount Wai-ale-ale in Hawaii has up to 350 rainy days a year.

Page 72 Listening Comprehension 1

Good morning. Today is Monday, the second of May. I'm Rob Murray with today's weather report.
It's sunny and the temperature is 16 degrees Celsius. There will be clouds tonight, and tomorrow we will have rain, with a temperature of 13 degrees. The rain will end tomorrow night. Wednesday will be sunny with temperatures in the high 20s.

Page 73 Listening Comprehension 2

Mike Lyons is a weather reporter, or "meteorologist," on Eyewitness News 25. He says when people recognize him, they often ask him questions about the weather. Most questions are easy for him to answer. But sometimes people ask him to do something about the weather.
For example, "My grass is brown. Can you make it rain?" He can't. He's happy when his weather forecast is correct. He, like other forecasters, sometimes make mistakes.
But Lyons suggests they may get help from Native Americans. Rain dances are the way the Indians pray for rain. Surprisingly, rain often follows these dances. Some people say that's because Native Americans understand nature.
To become a weather reporter you must study physics, mathematics, and geography. Lyons says it might be a good idea to add a course on Indian culture.

Unit 19 Sisters and Brothers

Page 74 Facts

A

1. A twin is one of two children who are born to the same mother at the same time.
2. A brother-in-law is the husband of your sister or the brother of your husband.
3. A person who doesn't have a sister or brother is called an only child.
4. A "soul sister" is a term used for someone who understands you.
5. A family tree tells about the relationships in a family.

Page 76 Listening Comprehension 1

The number of only children in the world is growing. But old and false ideas about them remain.

For example, many people believe that only children are lonely children. Dr. Harriet Mosatche says that this is not true. When only children have other children to play with, they aren't lonely. Another false belief is that only children don't play or work well with other children. Carol White writes for "Only Child" Newsletter. She says only children are often more social than some children with sisters or brothers. Only children don't have a choice. They have to make friends.

A third belief is that only children are spoiled, that they behave badly and expect to get everything they want. Dr. Mosatche explains that any child can be spoiled. It is how the parent raises the child that is important.

Page 77 Listening Comprehension 2

Charlotte, Anne, and Emily Bronte were important English writers. They were born in England in the early 1800s. There were six children in the family, but two died when they were very young. Charlotte was the oldest. She was born in 1816. Their brother, Patrick Branwell, was born in 1817, Emily was born in 1818, and Anne was born in 1820. Soon after Anne was born, their mother died and their aunt took care of them. Charlotte and Emily went to a school away from home, but they hated the school and returned before the year was over.

For the next several years the Bronte children were schooled at home. They made up games and told each other stories. They all sat around a square table.

In 1845, Charlotte found some poems Emily had written. Soon Charlotte, Emily, and Anne discovered that they all had been secretly writing poems. The sisters published their poems, but they didn't sell very well.

In 1847, Charlotte's novel Jane Eyre was published. It was a big success. Soon after, Anne published *Agnes Gray*, and Emily published *Wuthering Heights*. The sisters became successful and famous. The following year their brother Branwell died. Emily and Anne died soon after. Charlotte lived alone and continued to write.

Unit 20 Telephones

Page 78 Facts

A

1. Alexander Graham Bell invented the telephone.
2. The first cell phones appeared in the 1970s.
3. In the U.S., Europe, and Latin America, you can find business phone numbers in the Yellow Pages.
4. An operator can help you make a call.
5. When a phone is "dead," you can't get a dial tone.
6. The line is busy means someone is talking on the phone.

Page 80 Listening Comprehension 1

Man: Mary, listen to these messages. Let me know which sounds best.

Here's the first:

"Sorry we can't come to the phone. Please leave your name and a message. We'll get back to you soon."

And the second:

"Sorry. No one is here to take your call. Your call is very important to us. If you leave your name and a short message, we will get back to you shortly. Have a great day."

And the third one:

"Please leave your name, number, and a short message Thank you."

Woman: You know, John, I like the third one best. No one listens to your phone message. People just want to leave their message.

Man: I think you're right.

Page 81 Listening Comprehension 2

Hurry and buy our easy-to-use digital camera phones. Everyone needs one. They have a camera and a connection to the Internet. With this phone you can call or e-mail anyone anywhere. You can connect to another phone or to another computer. That means you can send a picture to a phone or a computer. So don't wait. Come to Computers Plus Store. We are located at 10 Main Street. There is a ten percent discount for the first hundred customers. This phone is only sold at Computers Plus. Our store opens at 9:00 AM. Don't miss this opportunity.

Unit 21 Urban and Rural areas

Page 82 Facts

A

1. Skyscrapers are tall buildings.
2. The tallest building in the world is in Taipei.
3. The Tiber, the Han, and the Seine are rivers that divide cities.
4. You can find the Grand Palace, floating markets, and a lot of traffic in Bangkok.
5. The Trevi Fountain and the Coliseum are in Rome.
6. Most people move from the countryside to the city for economic reasons.

Page 84 Listening Comprehension 1

Man: The apartment is large?
Woman: Yes. It's very large. It has three bedrooms, a dining room, and a modern eat-in kitchen.
Man: That sounds great. There's a nice view?
Woman: Yes. The living room faces the river. And there are two bathrooms and a terrace.
Man: Hmm. How far is it from the center of town?
Woman: About an hour by car.
Man: In traffic?
Woman: No. It's a lot longer in traffic. But that's okay. I really love the apartment.
Man: You're sure?
Woman: I'm sure.
Man: Well then, go for it.

Page 85 Listening Comprehension 2

Young woman: Do you live here, in the city?
Young man: Yes, I do and I'll never leave.
Young woman: Really? Why?
Young man: Everything happens here.
Young woman: I used to live here too, but my family moved to the country two years ago. It's great in the country.
Young man: It is?
Young woman: Sure. You can go hiking and fishing. And when I walk outside, I see trees and flowers. In the city I saw buildings, garbage, and people everywhere.

Young man:	What's wrong with people? I enjoy meeting all sorts of people.
Young woman:	People are fine, but you also have traffic, pollution, and cockroaches.
Young man:	At least it's not boring.
Young woman:	Listen. Come to my home this Sunday. You'll see it's not boring, and I promise you'll meet very interesting people and have some delicious fresh food.
Young man:	OK. It's a deal.

Unit 22 Vacations

Page 86 Facts

A

1. In 2000 and 2001 the most popular place for tourists to visit was France.
2. According to the World Tourist Organization, in 2020 the most popular place for tourists to visit will be China.
3. When people go camping, they sleep in tents.
4. The newest Disney theme park outside the United States is in Hong Kong.
5. When you visit famous or interesting places, you are sightseeing.
6. A gift you buy to remember a vacation is called a souvenir.

Page 88 Listening Comprehension 1

Dad:	Amy, are you ready for your camping trip?
Amy:	I think so Dad.
Dad:	Did you take a flashlight?
Amy:	Yes.
Dad:	How about extra batteries?
Amy:	No. I'll get some.
Dad:	Are you taking a can of beans?
Amy:	Yes. It's in my backpack.
Dad:	A box of matches?
Amy:	Uh-oh. I forgot them. I'll get a box.
Dad:	A pillow?
Amy:	No, but I don't need one.
Dad:	Then I guess you're all ready. Have a great time!
Amy:	Thanks Dad.

Page 89 Listening Comprehension 2

This month A to Z Tours offers two great trips. The first one is to Bryce Canyon National Park in the United States. And the second is to Cuzco and Machu Picchu in Peru.

Our trip to Bryce National Park begins in Las Vegas. A comfortable bus takes you to the park. At the park you will stay at a beautiful lodge. During the day you can join free tours of the area. You will see incredible rock formations. You will learn about the West and the Native Americans who lived there in the past.

Our second tour is to Machu Pichu and Cuzco in Peru. An air-conditioned bus will take you from Lima to the town of Cuzco. In Cuzco you will relax for a couple of days and then visit the ancient town of Machu Picchu. You can hike the Inca Trail or ride the railroad to Machu Picchu. We offer fun and adventure at a good price. Book with A to Z Tours today.

Unit 23 Women

Page 90 Facts

A

1. A sister, an aunt and a niece are all female relatives.
2. All of the following are women except a prince.
3. All of the following are famous women artists except Margaret Thatcher.
4. Women in the US won the right to vote in 1921. Women in Switzerland won the right to vote in 1971.
5. Women in New Zealand won the right to vote in 1893.
6. Ms. is the title for unmarried and married women.

Page 92 Listening Comprehension 1

1. Know the salaries of others in your field.
2. Before you go for an interview, write down things you have done at a job.
3. Tell your boss that the salary is important for you.
4. Get a good job title. It may be help for your next job.
5. Use facts to show what you did to save money at a job you had in the past.

Page 93 Listening Comprehension 2

Pretty women wonder where my secret lies.
I'm not cute or built to suit a fashion model's size
But when I start to tell them,
They think I'm telling lies.
I say,
It's in the reach of my arms,
The span of my hips,
The stride of my step,
The curl of my lips.
I'm a woman.

Unit 24 X-Rays and Bones

Page 94 Facts

A

1. Roentgen discovered X-rays in 1895.
2. The superhero with X-ray vision is Superman.
3. All the bones of the body together are the skeleton.
4. To wish an actor good luck before a play, we say, "Break a leg."
5. After you break an arm or leg, you usually wear a cast.
6. When someone gets hurt without anyone meaning it to happen, we call it an accident.

Page 96 Listening Comprehension 1

The black flag with a white skull and crossbones is called the "Jolly Roger." It is the pirate flag used in books and movies. It was the flag used by British and American pirates in the early 1700s. But other pirates used other flags.

Some flags showed skeletons, some showed hearts with blood pouring from them and an hourglass. All the flags tried to show one thing: the pirates weren't afraid of death.

Today we still see the skull and crossbones. It is a sign of poison or other dangers.

Page 97 Listening Comprehension 2

Wilhelm Roentgen was a German scientist. In 1895 he was working in his laboratory when he discovered X-rays by accident. A week later, he took an X-ray photograph of his wife's hand. It clearly showed her wedding ring and her bones. He sent the X-ray and a report about his work to the Medical Society of his city. Soon after, newspapers all over the world wrote about his discovery. Six years later, in 1901, Roentgen won the Nobel Prize in physics for his discovery.

X-rays are still a big part of all our lives. Doctors and dentists use X-rays to look inside the body. Airlines use X-rays to look inside baggage. And scientists use X-rays to study the stars.

How did Roentgen choose the name "X-ray"? He called these rays, "X" rays to show this was an unknown type of radiation. In mathematics, we usually use the letter "x" for unknown quantities. Many of Roentgen's friends wanted him to call them Roentgen rays, but he didn't. The name "X-ray" stayed and Roentgen's discovery changed the world.

Unit 25 Years ago: Childhood Memories

Page 98 Facts

A

1. Something for children to play with is called a toy.
2. Something children play with that looks like a small person is called a doll.
3. Worldwide sales of computer and video games in 2002 were over 10 billion dollars.
4. When children play "make-believe" games, they pretend to be someone they aren't.
5. When the puppet Pinocchio told a lie, his nose grew.
6. Most adults can't remember things that happened before the age of two and a half.

Page 100 Listening Comprehension 1

Girl 1: Who's up?
Boy: Bob.
Girl: What's the score?
Boy: It's three to two. They're winning and we have two outs.
Girl 1: Is Amy pitching?
Boy: Yeah.
Girl 1: She's good.
Boy: Oh. There's Bob. He's walking to the plate.
Umpire: STRIKE ONE!
Boy: Oh, no.
Girl 2: Way to go Amy!
Girl 1: You can do it Bob! Just keep your eye on the ball. Wow! Look at that ball fly. Run, Bob! Run!
Boy 2: It's a home run. Great! Hey, the score is three-three, and I'm up.
Girl 1: Good luck!

Page 101 Listening Comprehension 2

There's a special museum in North Wales called The Museum of Childhood Memories. At this museum everyone feels the magic of childhood. The museum contains nine rooms with about 2,000 items. Each room has a different theme. One room has teddy bears, nursery furniture, and push toys. In another room there are rocking horses and early bicycles and tricycles. There's a dollhouse room and a room with children's toy money boxes. Some of the exhibits are rare and the toys are very valuable, but the real value of the museum is that it brings everyone old and happy memories.

Unit 26 Zippers, Buttons, and Velcro: Clothes and Fashion

Page 102 Facts

A

1. The first zipper was shown at the Chicago World's Fair in the 1890s.
2. In 1952 the first Velcro company was started in Switzerland.
3. Fashionable clothes are in style.
4. All of the following are fabrics except jeans.
5. All of the following are clothes only for women except a vest.
6. A tailor alters clothes.

Page 104 Listening Comprehension 1

Woman 1: Hey Sara. How're you doing?
Woman 2: Great. How are you?
Woman 1: Fine....That sweater looks great.
Woman 2: Thanks.
Woman 1: I love that color on you. Is it new?
Woman 2: Uh-huh. It was a gift from my aunt..... I like your earrings.
Woman 1: You do? Thanks. I made them.
Woman 2: You're really talented.

Page 105 Listening Comprehension 2

The Story of the Zipper

Whitcomb Judson got a patent for the zipper in 1893. But this zipper didn't work and nobody wanted it. Judson showed it to millions of people at the Chicago World's Fair. He sold only 20 zippers.

In 1913 Gideon Sundback made a better zipper. But this zipper did not sell well either. Then ten years later, B.F. Goodrich became interested in the zipper. That's when zippers started to sell.

At that time B.F. Goodrich had a new product for the feet. He made rubber boots to protect people from the rain. He called these boots "galoshes." He liked the zipper and bought 150,000 for his galoshes. After that zippers sold everywhere.